Teacher Training in Physical Education

Teacher Training in Physical Education

Randhir Pal

Crescent

CRESCENT
PUBLISHING CORPORATION

[The responsibility for the facts stated, conclusions reached and plagiarism, if any, in this book is entirely that of the Author. And the Publisher bears no responsibility for them, whatsoever.]

Teacher Training in Physical Education

Edition : 2009

ISBN : 978-81-8342-110-2

Published by :

CRESCENT PUBLISHING CORPORATION
4831/24, Prahlad Street,
Ansari Road, Darya Ganj,
New Delhi - 110002
Ph. : 23272541, 23257835
Fax : 91-011-23257835
e-mail : campusbooks@hotmail.com

Printed at :

Roshan Offset Printers
Delhi

Preface

Physical education, as the name itself suggests, refers to a discipline or a programme of activity, which aims to propagate the development and knowledge about the physical body. And indeed, physical education, a vital and integral part of general education, combines such objectives as development of motor skills for general activities as sports, games and gymnastics, body development and fitness, knowledge and understanding of sports, exercise, health and safety, and even development of emotional and social behaviour. As disciplines go, physical education, just like any other subject, requires professionals and teachers who are trained thoroughly within the rigmarole of the subject.

This book in the encyclopaedia on physical education is meant to serve as a manual which looks into the issue of training professionals in the field of physical education. As the awareness and stress placed on physical education increases, the scope and complexity of physical education has also increased. As a consequence, teachers today have to be not just familiar with what entails the subject, but have to also been attained into the constantly evolving nuances of the subject.

The book looks into teacher training in physical education in both a panoramic as well as an in-depth manner. Delineating the relevance of the subject, it explores in detail the aspects of the sub-disciplines studied in physical education, such as exercise physiology, motor learning, kinesiology, biomechanics, sociology of sport, etc. The effort is to entrench the readers thoroughly into the working of the subject, and explores current social and health contexts which are crucial to training professionals within this field. With its emphasis on a research-oriented and incisively critiqued content, and erudition combined with insight, it is hoped the book serves well for the readers.

Randhir Pal

Contents

1

Vision for Effective Physical Education Training

The most important aspect of physical education is the direct bearing it has on children's physical, mental, and social wellbeing. The child who is well educated physically is likely to become a healthy adult who is motivated to remain healthy. Although adults are often well informed about health and pursue healthy life-styles that include good nutrition, exercise, physical activity, and fitness, their children's physical health and well-being are frequently a cause for concern.

Recognizing the threat of a sedentary life-style inherent in postindustrial work patterns, large numbers of adults can be found jogging, walking, eating healthy foods, and seeking out ways to incorporate movement and activity into their daily routines. But at the same time alarming numbers of children and youths, often lacking appropriate adult supervision, can be found in front of television sets on sunny weekday afternoons munching on snack foods. This problem is compounded by approaches to physical education that have traditionally emphasized competition, games, sports, and native athletic ability, favoring those who are most talented and leaving the less able to view themselves as outsiders who will never make the grade. Our society can no longer afford that approach.

A second reason for the importance of physical education today is its direct link with academic learning. The healthy, physically active child is more likely to be academically motivated, alert, and successful. In the preschool and primary years, there are direct links between active play, physical agility and coordination, and academic success. As children grow older and enter adolescence, healthy physical activity becomes integral to their self-concept and their ability to take on new intellectual, social, and emotional challenges. Throughout, physical education promotes the social skills and cooperation that are increasingly viewed by educators today as essential for success in school. Just as any well-planned academic curriculum takes into account a wide range of learning modes and styles, the physical education curriculum, emphasizes a variety of cognitive, affective, and psychomotor teaching and learning strategies.

A physically educated person is one who has mastered the necessary movement skills to participate confidently in many different forms of physical activity, values physical fitness, and understands that both are intimately related to health and well-being. The most basic element of a child's development is learning to move. Even before birth children begin learning to move and learning through movement. The process continues throughout childhood and early adolescence. Movement skills are central to physical education at all grade levels.

Physical education addresses the child's fundamental need for regular physical activity to remain healthy and promotes many of the attitudes and behaviors that reduce health risks, including development of an understanding of the need for appropriate nutrition and exercise. A quality physical education program can motivate students to maintain healthy eating habits and regular physical activity. A well-planned physical education program guides students to becoming motivated to attain optimum health through regular use of new knowledge and skills.

A slang expression, couch potato, aptly describes someone who is the opposite of a physically educated person: unfit, inactive, and oblivious to the basic principles of staying fit and healthy. Ironically, some adults who today lack fitness and health were yesterday's child and teenage star athletes. In their youth they may have been successful in a highly competitive sport-almost always with one primary goal, winning. Other adults, now leading inactive, unhealthy life-styles, may once have been the opposite. Lacking athletic talent, they may have been overlooked or neglected in physical education classes.

Many different elements of age appropriate physical activity and instruction help to develop a commitment to lifelong health, physical activity, and physical education. All children and youths, regardless of their athletic talents, should have a variety of opportunities to participate in physical education and enrich their lives through physical activity.

Goals of Physical Education

A comprehensive, articulated physical education system helps children and youths achieve three goals. Within each goal appropriate disciplines are addressed to support the knowledge, skills, and attitudes desired for every student. The three goals are equally important; each interacts continually with the others in a well-planned program.

— *Goal 1: Movement Skills and Movement Knowledge*

Disciplines:

1. Motor Learning
2. Biomechanics
3. Exercise Physiology and Health-related Physical Fitness

— Goal: Self-Image and Personal Development

Disciplines:

1. Human Growth and Development
2. Psychology

3. Aesthetics

— Goal: Social Development

Disciplines:

1. Sociology
2. Historical Perspectives

Skill and Content Areas

The following skill and content areas support the goals of physical education and are introduced at appropriate ages and grade levels. In addition to developing skills in these various areas, students should be encouraged to acquire understanding and knowledge about the content and skills. They should be able to grasp the why as well as the how and to understand that the content areas are a vehicle for developing and refining the skills.

Skill Areas

— *Sensorimotor and perceptual motor*. Examples: kinesthetic, visual, tactile, auditory

— *Locomotor*. Examples: walking, running, jumping, hopping, galloping, skipping

— *Nonlocomotor*. Examples: swinging/swaying, bending/stretching, pushing/pulling, twisting/turning

— *Balance*. Examples: static: stunts, balance equipment; dynamic: tricycle, unicycle, scooter, beams

— *Eye-hand coordination.* Examples: gross motor: throwing, catching, bouncing; fine motor: pouring, clapping, cutting, grasping

— *Eye-foot coordination*. Examples: kicking, trapping, dribbling, punting, rhythmic movement

— *General coordination*. Examples: swinging, climbing, sliding, jumping rope, tumbling

— *Creative movement*. Examples: rhythmic walking, swaying, moving to music, mirroring movement

Content Areas

— Rhythms and Dance o Individual and Dual Sports

— Aquatics o Team Sports

— Combatives (e.g., self-defense o Mechanics of Body Movement and fencing)

— Outdoor Education Dynamic Health

— Gymnastics and Tumbling

These skill and content areas are the basis of physical education. For example, developing a sense of rhythm helps children do better in a variety of activities and enhances a sense of flow and coordination. At all levels of the physical education curriculum, the skill areas are taught and reinforced through the content.

Cognitive learning is an inherent part of the skill and content areas. For example, students learn the application of Newton's laws in developing rotational skills, balance, and spin. This knowledge helps to reinforce and strengthen their understanding of the skills and their ability to use them. Throughout the physical education curriculum, children should be encouraged to observe their own and others' behavior and to process information. Although children do learn through trial and error, they also benefit from guided discovery and development of an understanding of skills and content.

Myths and Vision

The vision of physical education and the physically educated individual presented in this chapter counteracts common myths about physical education:

Myth. Physical education is intended to help students achieve excellence in games and sports.

Vision. Physical education is a multifaceted process that teaches a wide range of skills and activities with the aim of the students' becoming physically educated, physically fit, able to enjoy a variety of physical activities, and committed to lifelong health and physical well-being. It is a continuing process of articulated, sequential development of skills, talents, attitudes, and behaviors.

Myth. Physical education is not an integral part of the school's curriculum. It is a frill.

Vision. Physical education is closely connected to and supports the other disciplines. Physical education is an integral component of the school curriculum. It involve students directly in thinking, creating meaning, and learning how to learn.

Myth. Physical education focuses on the more athletically gifted.

Vision. All children have the potential to become physically educated, and an effective physical education program will reach all children regardless of their talents, skills, or limitations.

Myth. Physical education should be similar to training-highly skill- and drill-oriented. It should be mainly a mechanical process.

Vision. In physical education emphasis must be placed on a broad spectrum of learning and personal development. Learning involves thinking and feeling, being active and processing information, not just using skills. Education encompasses much more than training.

Myth. Children should carry out a variety of physical fitness activities but do not need to understand why they are doing so.

Vision. Learning cognitively is as important to physical education as learning specific movement skills. Students need to know why they are learning skills in physical education and how they are benefiting personally. Then they will be more likely to accept responsibility for improving skills on their own and enjoying the benefits of physical education over the long term.

Myth. Physical education programs may be detrimental to doing one's best in a particular activity. It is important to focus on a specific activity (or sport) in order to do really well.

Vision. A well-planned, comprehensive physical education system helps children and youths develop all their abilities and talents rather than focus exclusively on a narrow range. Because children change and grow over time, they should be encouraged to become well rounded. They should be encouraged to become proficient in and appreciate a wide variety of physical activities from which they can choose wisely.

Myth. Because there are always winners and losers in games and sports, physical education must emphasize competition to prepare children for participation in the real world.

Vision. Although teachers are aware of the nature of competition, they do not require higher levels of competition from children before they are ready. Further, competition can take different forms. Activities in physical education programs may emphasize self-improvement, participation, and cooperation instead of winning or losing.

Competitive Aspect of Physical Education

Excessive emphasis on the competitive aspect of sports, games, and athletic achievement conflicts with the goals of physical education.

However, normal competition is an inherent part of American life and can be an element in a child's intrinsic motivation to do his or her best in any physical activity.

A common mistake is to emphasize competition too much while children are still quite young. Children are able to create their own competition in normal play. In early childhood children should be encouraged to recognize the intrinsic reward of doing one's personal best. Only at about the age of ten or eleven are they ready physiologically, socially, and emotionally to participate in other levels of competitive activities.

A program oriented to the success of every child provides a nonthreatening environment in which a child is never subjected to the humiliation of being chosen last or being dropped from a team. Attention should be focused on the uniqueness and abilities of each person.

Neither winning nor losing is the crux of physical education. What matters is that competition equates with making the most of one's physical potential and capabilities in a positive, meaningful way. The goal of the physical educator should be not to identify winners but to make winners of ordinary students.

PHYSICAL EDUCATION AND HEALTH EDUCATION

A well-planned physical education program is one component of a comprehensive school health system. That system, which comprises an organized set of policies, procedures, and activities designed to protect and promote the health and well-being of students and staff, includes the following components:

— Health Education

— Physical Education

— Health Services

— Nutrition Services

— Psychological and Counseling Services

— Safe and Healthy School Environment

— Health Promotion for Staff

— Parent and Community Involvement

As two components in a comprehensive school health system, physical education and health education should complement each other. However, the ways in which they are separate and distinct must be recognized. Health education focuses on four unifying ideas of health literacy. Health literacy is "the capacity of an individual to obtain, interpret, and understand basic health information and services and the competence to use such information and services in ways which are health-enhancing." The four unifying ideas are the following:

— Acceptance of personal responsibility for lifelong health
— Respect for and promotion of the health of others
— An understanding of the process of growth and development
— Informed use of health-related information, products, and services

Physical education focuses on three goals:

— movement skills and movement knowledge;
— self-image and personal development; and
— social development.

Where physical education differs most distinctly from health education is in the emphasis that physical education places on teaching students how to move.

Development of a Physically Educated Person

The development of a physically educated person can be compared with the growth of a tree. The roots of the tree correspond to the preschool and primary levels. At this point children are learning the fundamentals of physical education, becoming more skillful, and deriving pleasure from learning new skills through experience with the various content areas. Three fundamentals of physical education that correspond to learning letters in reading and learning numbers in mathematics are central to these levels:

— Locomotion-moving the body from one place to another

— Nonlocomotion-remaining in place and maintaining balance while moving parts of the body
— Object manipulation-including manipulating objects with parts of the body

At the preschool and primary levels, development of physical and motor fitness attributes is emphasized, including agility, flexibility, and coordination. This level emphasizes such basic skills as walking, running, hopping, jumping, sliding, galloping, skipping, catching, throwing, kicking, balancing, bending, and stretching. Also important are such fitness attributes as cardiorespiratory fitness and muscular strength and endurance.

The trunk of the tree corresponds to the upper elementary years. At this level children begin to combine the fundamental skills they have learned in the preschool and primary years and apply and refine the skills in new experiences. At the upper levels of the tree, including the middle school years, children are becoming independent, self-directed learners. They are beginning to internalize the principles of physical education from the earlier grades into a personal commitment to a healthy life-style and physical activity. They participate regularly in a variety of physical activities, take pleasure in both group and individual activities, and have begun to formulate a goal of lifelong health. Throughout, the process engages all aspects of learning: cognitive ("I know"); affective ("I feel"); and psychomotor ("I experience and do").

As the tree branches out at the upper levels, high school students are able to choose and participate freely in team sports, individual sports, aquatics, dance, combatives, fitness, tumbling and gymnastics, and other specific aspects of the physical education curriculum. This is an appropriate time for specializing in particular activities, a time when skills learned at the earlier levels become more meaningful and pleasurable in ways that are both satisfying and complex.

Physical Education Curriculum Development

Throughout the kindergarten through grade twelve curriculum, all three goals of physical education are addressed, together with their respective disciplines. There is a flow of learning from one goal to another and from one grade level to another. Because movement and activity are central to physical education, the goal of movement skills and movement knowledge is the key to a well-planned program.

True comprehensiveness can be achieved, however, only through a focus on all three goals. Within each goal the appropriate disciplines support the knowledge, skills, and attitudes desired for every student. The disciplines are an important part of the knowledge base of physical education, guiding what is taught and when. They provide instructors with both a rationale for the instructional program and specific content.

Movement Knowledge

Students need to develop effective motor skills and to understand the fundamentals of movement by practicing and analyzing purposeful movement. The most basic element of the student's learning experience in physical education is learning how to move. The physical education curriculum begins, therefore, by addressing the primary goal of achieving movement skills and movement knowledge. A comprehensive physical education program guides each student in the development of motor skills that allow the student to:

1. Move in a variety of ways.
2. Learn effective and efficient movement appropriate to the student's changing needs.
3. Understand the fundamentals of movement.
4. Appreciate the aesthetics of creative movement.
5. Enjoy movement for movement's sake.

6. Develop all the skills needed to select appropriate activities to develop and maintain a high level of health-related physical fitness.

Movement is the primary medium through which the physical educator reaches and teaches the whole child. Emphasis should be placed on guiding children to discover what they can do. They need to develop proficiency in movement skills so that physical activity will be a successful and enjoyable experience that enhances self-image. Moreover, they should have opportunities to participate in expressive and creative movement leading to greater self-realization and personal satisfaction. Experiences in physical education can play a powerful role in influencing a student's self-image, which, in turn, influences how that student will feel about continuing (or avoiding) participation in physical activity.

Motor Learning

Motor learning and motor development together are the basis for how motor skills are learned and what they look like. These concepts can be described in terms of the learner and the learning environment. Motor learning involves development of locomotor skills (e.g., walking, running, hopping, jumping) and nonlocomotor skills (e.g., balancing, bending, twisting, reaching, stretching) and an understanding of the qualities of time, space, force, and flow applicable to those skills. It also involves object manipulation, such as catching, throwing, kicking, and juggling. Motor learning enables students to master skills in order to perform them consistently and well. It involves feedback, judgment, and trial and error. An example is learning how to take aim and hit a mark. Motor learning is also progressive-for example, learning how to bounce a ball with control before learning to dribble.

Motor development refers to what the skills and activities look like in terms of their qualities. Skills and activities can be performed in isolation or as part of a more complex dance, game, sport, or other performance. Motor learning is the how of what students learn, and motor development is the what. In the elementary grades it is particularly important that children receive, interpret, and respond to visual, auditory, tactile, and kinesthetic stimuli for sensorimotor and perceptual motor feedback. Perceptual motor development is a crucial need in the early grades, influencing more than just the child's ability to move. It also has an important influence on readiness for learning.

Biomechanics

Biomechanics is the science that examines the internal and external forces acting on a human body and the effects they produce. It involves the study of how the body moves and how such movement is influenced by gravity, friction, and the laws of motion. Knowing how and why movement occurs and whether it is efficient assists in problem solving and enhances understanding of movement and motor skills. This understanding enables students to modify their performance for skill improvement and determine the most appropriate technique for each motor skill.

Key terms include Newton's laws of motion, center of gravity, force projection and absorption, buoyancy, spin, rotational mechanics, levers, vectors, and motion. Through experimentation or guided discovery, students learn that by applying biomechanical principles to physical activity, they can improve their skills and performance.

Personal Development

Human Growth and Development

Children experience the stages of growth and development at different rates. When they learn that individuals are not automatically considered wrong or bad if they develop more slowly or more rapidly than their peers, they are better prepared to accept individual differences. At the same time certain aspects of physical development are relatively common at specific age and grade levels. An understanding of the body-type variations of endomorph (fat), mesomorph (muscular), and ectomorph (thin) can help students accept capabilities and limitations that may be a function of body type. Therefore, an understanding of developmentally appropriate activities is necessary.

Psychology

Positive emotional development is closely related to good feelings resulting from movement in physical education activities. One aspect of positive emotional development is learning to acknowledge, accept, and appreciate differences between oneself and others with regard to abilities and achievement. Self-acceptance, which is enhanced as students take pride in personal excellence and try to improve their performance, is closely connected with developing a sense of personal responsibility. By overcoming physical challenges and other obstacles at each level of development, students acquire the confidence they need to progress further and to take on new challenges.

Aesthetics

Physical education reinforces self-confidence and self-image by providing students with a sense of accomplishment and aesthetic pleasure in mastering and applying movement skills. This effect is not limited to superior levels but can happen at all levels of competence. Participating in physical activity helps students develop a heightened awareness of how the body feels in movement, how it can be trained to move more efficiently, and why it needs regular vigorous exercise to achieve and maintain good health. In turn, a healthy body moves more gracefully and effectively for longer periods of time.

The healthy person feels good about moving and enjoys a sense of exhilaration in movement. Across the ages every culture has expressed itself through dance and movement. The philosophy, art, life-style, political life, and religion of diverse cultures have all been translated into movement in rituals, games, or dances. All are potential means of achieving creative selfexpression.

Social Development

Students develop appropriate social behaviors by working independently and with others during planned physical activity. Participating in physical activity as a member of a group is central to children's acceptance of responsibility for their health and physical wellbeing and a lifelong appreciation of physical activity. Through guided experiences all students should develop the skills needed to participate with others in a productive manner not only in physical education activities but in all other aspects of social interaction as well. Working with another student or in small groups, students can support each other in meeting challenges, testing each other's skills, and living, working, and playing together harmoniously. They learn that effective group work depends on cooperation and fair competition. They also learn to assess situations and to identify and solve problems.

When competition is kept in perspective so that the students can achieve their full potential, they learn to value fair play and control their emotions. By emphasizing fair competition and good sportsmanship, physical education contributes to the students' development of a personal code of ethics that leads to making morally responsible decisions. The acquisition of positive social skills also contributes to the mental health and well-being of each student by combating risk factors for substance abuse and other social problems. All students can learn positive social skills, which must be modeled daily by instructional leaders.

Sociology

Sociology, a dynamic process by which the culture and norms of a society are transmitted, includes learning the society's norms, roles, values, and expectations as well as studying human relationships and social behavior.

In physical education sociology relates to developing and applying positive social norms and values not only to physical education activities but also to intramural athletics and other school activities. The learning and acceptance of social norms help students to develop an acceptance not just of rules but of the need for fairness and equity. Sociology also emphasizes learning to respect others, appreciate the diversity of our society, and recognize the importance of understanding other cultures. Closely associated with these aspects of social interaction is the need to understand the development of appropriate social behavior and etiquette in a variety of settings on and off the playing field.

Historical Perspectives

Physical education has the longest history of all educational efforts. Understanding history contributes to both the student's and the instructor's awareness of the rationale underlying physical education today. Physical education has changed considerably over the years. During the early Middle Ages, for example, physical development was considered secondary to development of the mind. With the Renaissance, however, came a new emphasis on the development of the whole person. In the eighteenth century the importance of developing both a sound body and a sound mind was emphasized, reflecting a return to the philosophy of ancient Greece.

Even in our own century, numerous trends have affected physical education. Different games, sports, and activities have been in favor at different times. Nevertheless, the essentials of movement and coordination underlying these games are often the same (e.g., combatives). Over a period of decades, emphasis has shifted from wrestling and boxing to the martial arts.

Our contemporary awareness of the importance of all aspects of health (physical, mental, and social) has led to a comprehensive view of physical education emphasizing development of a healthy body, mind, and spirit, together with a focus on the individual's role in contributing to the health of society in general. Thus, physical education teaches all children to enjoy being physically active to the extent that they are able, resolve conflicts peacefully, and prepare for a long, healthy, active life.

2

Quality Instruction in Physical Education

To create high expectations for quality instruction, physical education teachers must continually strive to improve their effectiveness.

Model Lesson

Teachers create an optimal learning environment and an effective learning experience for their students through careful planning. The heart of effective instruction is the actual physical education lesson. Throughout the lesson the teacher should maintain an orderly, safe, businesslike atmosphere and have clear expectations for the behavior and achievement of students. The teacher implements the lesson plan and makes adjustments as necessary for students not experiencing success or not participating.

Each day should begin with a variety of warm-up exercises involving the muscles to be used in the instructional phase and lasting one or two minutes. All students should be expected to perform the exercises to the best of their ability. However, adjustments may need to be made to deal with individual abilities. The teacher supervises the students, explains the purpose of each exercise, and provides corrective or positive feedback.

Warm-up is followed by the instructional phase. At this point the teacher explains the purpose of the main activity, which will include demonstrations and explanations. Then comes the activity phase. During the activity phase each student is engaged in skill-learning time, with enough correct practice trials being provided during class time to acquire the desired skill. Activities should be designed to keep to a minimum the amount of time spent waiting in line and moving between activities. Equipment should be deployed efficiently. Whenever possible, students should be placed in cooperative learning groups.

When working with individual students, the teacher should personalize instruction by using the student's name and giving feedback equally to boys and girls and to high achievers and low achievers in appropriate ways. At the end of the class, the teacher should provide a chance for discussion or processing of the lesson, encouraging the students to review the objectives or key points. In this way students can see relationships, attitudes, values, and other insights related to the lesson, and teachers can adjust the lessons for optimal learning the next day.

Components of a Model Physical

Variety of Strategies

Teachers should use a variety of teaching styles, including teacherdirected and student-initiated learning, to satisfy the learning styles of individual students and stimulate higher levels of thinking and creativity. Teaching styles might include command, practice, self-check, guided discovery, student-designed and student-initiated teaching, and selfteaching. Teachers should also employ a variety of instructional approaches, including competency-based learning, contract learning, drill, information processing, lecture, mastery learning, programmed instruction, and role-playing.

Especially appropriate for physical education instruction is cooperative learning. Assigning students to small learning groups (three to six members each) allows teachers and students to achieve a variety of goals, both social and cognitive. In addition, research has shown that cooperative learning produces higher achievement; improves cross-ethnic friendships and social skills; enhances self-image; and promotes greater interdependence, improved role-taking abilities (e.g., leadership), and a better classroom climate.

The first step in cooperative learning is the formation of heterogeneous teams. The size of each team will vary according to the activity; however, groups of three to six students (mixed as to ability, race, and gender) have proven to be most successful. After the teams have been formed, students need activities for team building and time to practice and receive feedback on appropriate social skills. The specifics of cooperative learning lessons depend to a great extent on which method among many different cooperative learning approaches is chosen. However, the teacher must ensure positive interdependence and both individual and group rewards. A team can succeed only if all members are interdependent in their contributions toward a common goal.

Instructional Media and Resources

Many types of instructional media and resources, as distinct from equipment for games and sports, are available to aid the physical education teacher. In addition to textbooks, workbooks, and more conventional printed materials, resources include films, filmstrips, videos, laser discs, CD-Rom, and large-screen projections of televised or videotaped images. Physical education teachers should look for ways not only to incorporate a variety of instructional media into their teaching but also to make sure that the media are available and are included in the overall budget for physical education.

Examples abound of appropriate instructional technology in physical education. Heart monitors can provide students with feedback on their heart rate while they are performing cardiovascular exercises. In addition, camcorders and video cameras can be used to capture students' performances for skill or strategy analysis. Computers can aid the teacher in the production of task cards or skill cards and can also be used to provide information and instructional modules to individuals or groups. When connected to laser disc players, videocassette players and other peripheral devices can capture students' interest through multimedia presentations.

A wide variety of computer software programs are available that lead students through tutorials on various sport or fitness concepts, offering both instruction and assessment procedures. An interactive laser-disc system can present students with information generated by computer software linked to the laser-disc player at different points in the tutorial. The player, instructed by the computer software, displays the appropriate live-action example. Interactive programs offer students a considerable amount of control over their own learning and the topics they wish to explore. Technology is also very useful in the assessment process.

Instructional Strategies to Meet Special Needs

Every physical education class includes students who are high achievers; those who are low achievers; and those, the majority, in the middle. Effective instructional strategies take into account the diverse needs of what are often very heterogeneous groups. All students, not just a select few, should receive positive feedback and reinforcement from the instructor or other students; and all should have opportunities to be involved.

Gender Equity

Federal law and California law require that students of both sexes be treated equally in integrated physical education classes. All students, male and female, should be given the teacher's attention and feedback on an equal basis and should be called on equally to demonstrate new skills. The teacher should also discipline males and females equally.

Students with Disabilities

Some students will come to physical education with motor or perceptual deficits; others, with more severe disabilities. Successful participation in physical activities by students with disabilities depends on the teacher's attitude and skill in providing instruction and support to all students. The teacher should continually encourage all students to learn and experience maximum enjoyment in physical education by understanding students' specific needs and encouraging students who are not disabled to accept and support those who are.

Children with disabilities, whether they are identified as needing special education and related services or not, have the right to a modification of the regular program. Further, under Section 504 of the Rehabilitation Act of 1973, Amendments of 1991 (Public Law 102-42), and the American with Disabilities Act of 1990 (Public Law 101-336), such children may not be discriminated against by school personnel. Service delivery options that must be made available to all children with disabilities are modified general physical education, specially designed physical education, and adapted physical education; direct services; collaboration; and consultation.

In some instances an individualized education program team at the school (e.g., the physical education teacher, the adapted physical education specialist, special education teachers, administrators, parents, and ancillary personnel, such as occupational therapists and physical therapists) will determine that the appropriate least-restrictive environment for a physical education program for students with disabilities is the general education class.

To accommodate such students, the physical education instructor may have to make modifications and interventions. In collaboration with the adapted physical education specialist, special education teachers, and ancillary personnel, the physical education teacher can modify instruction to accommodate students with disabilities without diminishing the value of the class for those without disabilities.

Problem-solving skills and modified approaches to movement can be offered at the elementary level; flexible or optional unit schedules, at the middle or junior high school level; and elective or selective programs, at the senior high school level.

Teaching methods can be adapted to meet the needs of students through provision of a direct tutor, a buddy system that pairs students with disabilities with other students, peer tutoring, task cards or individualized learning packets, circuit or station setups, contracts or independent student programs, and other approaches. Other adaptations might include:

— Basing evaluation on the student's potential and on pretest and posttest comparison rather than on standardized scores

— Basing measurement on what the student with disabilities is able to do rather than on what the student is not able to do

— Applying decathlon-scoring approaches to enable students with disabilities to compete for points against records that are appropriate to their physical status

— Providing specific devices or adapting equipment to aid in the manipulation of objects or oneself

— Using a larger ball or larger pieces of equipment to make the activity easier or to slow the pace of the activity

— Using a smaller, lighter ball or striking implement (plastic or soft ball or plastic bats) or an object that is easier to handle (beanbag or softball)

— Adding more players to a team to reduce the amount of activity and responsibility of any individual player

— Assigning playing positions according to the abilities of the students with disabilities Permitting the substitution or interchange of duties during participation

— Limiting play areas if students' movement capabilities are restricted

The physical education teacher should seek out opportunities for informal talks with the adapted physical education specialist or special education teacher to develop methods for working with students with disabilities. When these students cannot participate safely and successfully in the physical education program and when interventions have been ineffective, the specialist in adapted physical education must take a more active role. Use of the individualized education plan process for special education may be required.

Differences in Language or Communication

Different types of instructional approaches will also be needed for students with limited proficiency in English or other communication problems. Bilingual interpreters or instructors skilled in sign language may be needed. For non-English speakers, information offered in their native language helps develop not just understanding but a positive attitude toward the information.

For teachers who do not speak a second language and for students who are limited-English proficient, sheltered instruction is another approach that can be used. Sheltered instruction provides students with a variety of interactive and multimodal means to accessing information. In sheltered instruction the language demands of the lesson can be modified through such techniques as clear enunciation, controlled vocabulary, fewer idioms, and such contextual cues as gestures, facial expressions, demonstrations, props, visuals, and overhead transparencies. Cooperative learning has also proved effective in teaching students at various levels of English proficiency because high levels of interaction are associated with enhanced learning of content and English.

Assessment of Students

Several different forms of assessment can be used to measure student progress and achievement in physical education: student portfolios, teacher observations, performance tests, open-ended questions, interviews, exhibitions, and cooperative group projects. The results of these assessments demonstrate how children use skills, solve movement problems, and progress over time. Assessment can also reveal the effectiveness of the instructional program and provide insight into how physical education teachers can make learning more meaningful. Quality assessment informs students, teachers, and parents about each student's progress toward the yearly learning expectations. Student profile information should be documented and maintained to monitor students' progress from year to year. At the beginning of each term, the teacher should assess each student to determine appropriate student expectations, instructional starting points, and grouping approaches. However, the entire evaluation process should be viewed as a means rather than as an end.

Educators in all disciplines are moving increasingly toward authentic assessment, an evaluation process that can contribute to a lively, active, and exciting learning experience for students. Authentic assessment engages students in challenges requiring the application of skills, knowledge, and attitudes. It requires students to explain or demonstrate how they can use what they have learned. The assessment, relevant feedback, and results are reported to each student immediately, together with a focus on the student's strengths and aspects of performance that may need improvement. Historically, physical education has always assessed fitness and motor skills. The challenge now is to find authentic assessment instruments for the cognitive and affective domains.

A variety of methods can be used, including written tests; videotaped performances of skills; cooperative learning activities; individual, small-group, and class projects; problem-solving tasks; small-group and class discussions; task cards; work sheets; contracts; small-group and class projects; and homework. Self-assessment is another means of providing students with information about their performance. Students can apply self-evaluation when given lists of performance objectives and directed to judge their own achievement. This procedure can be facilitated by the videotaping of the student's performance for follow-up viewing by the student. On a higher level self-assessment can offer opportunities for students to establish personal goals and make critical and valid evaluations as they monitor their progress.

Establishing personal goals and practicing self-assessment should be an integral part of the students' learning experience in physical education. Self-assessment also helps motivate students to assume responsibility for their own learning. Peer assessment, which can be carried out by learners in pairs or groups, is an effective evaluation method for sixth grade or above.

As students develop peer assessment skills, they learn the importance of giving and receiving support and constructive feedback. In peer assessment the student evaluator compares and contrasts another student's performance with the criteria established by the teacher. The results can be communicated orally or through the use of a task card, rating scale, or checklist. Peer assessment can be done live or can be videotaped. Grades should bear a close relationship to the course goals and learning expectations. Course grades should not be used to report such elements as attendance, cleanliness, personality, punctuality, and wearing apparel. Assessment should require students to:

— Demonstrate an understanding of the application of information in new and familiar tasks.

— Explain why and how rather than merely perform movement.

— Integrate and connect understanding, analyze self-performances, observe others, and experiment with this knowledge.

— Demonstrate imagination, persistence, and creativity and show a capability for problem solving.

The physical education grade, based on the individual's progress toward the course objectives, should be included in the high school grade point average along with all other grades and should be accepted by colleges and universities. Grading based on the achievement of clearly stated goals and objectives emphasizes what students know and can do. One form of grading involves an assessment instrument that describes a standard against which a piece of work or skill is judged. The assessment instrument tells the student what has to be accomplished. For the evaluation to be valid and fair, the student and evaluator must share a common understanding of what is to be accomplished. Throughout the semester students should be kept informed of their grades. Before any evaluation they should be provided with enough time for instruction and practice.

Performance Standards for Student Work

The following is a suggested example of generic performance standards for students' work at each of six possible performance levels that can be applied to any task or group of tasks. The three types of performances in physical education in which a student can achieve include purpose of task, understanding, and personal and social growth.

Level	Standard to be achieved for performance at specified level
6	*Achieves purpose of the task fully while insightfully interpreting, extending beyond the task, or raising provocative questions*

— Possesses motor skills, knowledge, and under-standing requisite to success in physical activities and maintenance of a healthy life-style
— Demonstrates skills, knowledge, and understanding
— Models equitable and ethical behaviors toward others

5 *Accomplishes the purposes of the task*

— Possesses the motor skills, knowledge, and understanding needed for success in physical activities
— Selects activity appropriate to personal capabilities
— Shows ability to accept and respect achievement level of self and others

4 *Completes purpose of the task substantially*

— Displays movement proficiency with limited transfer of learning to other activities
— Demonstrates willingness to experience new activities
— Applies rules, vocabulary, strategy, and etiquette most of the time in activity

3 *Purpose of the task not fully elaboration; some strategies perhaps ineffectual or inappropriate; assumptions about the purposes perhaps flawed*

— Movements more consistent but unreliable
— Demonstrates limited acceptance of individual differences in self or others
— Interacts positively most of the time with others in small groups

2. *Important purposes of the task not achieved; redirection of work perhaps needed; completion affected by approach to task*

— Movements inconsistent and unreliable
— Ongoing affirmation required to attend to the task
— Teacher direction required for basic cooperation

1 *Purposes of the task not accomplished*

— Shows little evidence of ability to control or replicate a movement
— Is unable to verbalize needs
— Displays unstable, inappropriate, aggressive social behavior

Criteria for Instructional Resources in Physical Evaluating Education

Content of Instructional Resources

All the goals should be addressed, with support from their respective disciplines. Resources should present physical education as a comprehensive, sequential system that promotes the physical, mental, emotional, and social well-being of each student. The presentation of resources should be open and engaging, and vocabulary should be incorporated to facilitate understanding for both teachers and students.

Students should be encouraged to acquire understanding and knowledge about the content and skills of physical education. They should be able to grasp the why as well as the how of what they are doing.

They should also understand that the content areas (rhythm and dance, aquatics, combatives, outdoor education, team sports, individual and dual sports, tumbling and gymnastics, and fitness) are vehicles for developing and refining skills. The content and skill areas are the basis of physical education.

The idea of competition should be introduced gradually in instructional resources as in the overall physical education program itself.

Students should understand that competition equates with making the most of one's physical potential and capabilities in a positive, meaningful way.

Access to Instructional Resources

Instructional resources in physical education should recognize cultural diversity and reflect strategies that research and practice have shown to be successful in engaging all students in learning. For all students to participate fully, tasks and activities should be made accessible to all students through a variety of approaches.

Woven throughout, for example, should be a multicultural perspective promoting respect for the dignity and worth of all people regardless of their differences and building on the knowledge, attitudes, beliefs, and cultural and linguistic foundation that students bring to class. The instructional resources should include activities for all students, including students with disabilities.

Instructional guides should provide ways to make instruction for limited-English-proficient (LEP) students comprehensible, age-appropriate, and commensurate with their academic backgrounds. The provision of glossaries and summaries of key concepts in the students' primary language is one way of giving LEP students access to the physical education curriculum. The format of resources-including clear headings, subheadings, illustrations, photographs, graphs, and charts, all clearly labeled-can greatly increase the likelihood that all students will understand basic concepts. Such conventions are critical for students with special needs, such as LEP students.

The instructional resources should provide teachers with general and lesson-specific advice to support the learning of all students, including ways to:

— Connect the students' daily experiences with classroom activities.

— Encourage students to recognize and value the points of view and experiences of others where appropriate.

— Use peer support and cooperative learning groups.

— Use activities in which students experience both challenge and success.

— Make appropriate use of technology.

— Emphasize clearly that a desirable goal is for each individual to participate in a variety of pleasurable physical activities and to maintain an active life-style.

Support for the Teacher

Suggestions to aid the teacher should be based on current research on learning styles and effective instruction. Instructional resources should include, within the units of instruction, descriptions of the key goals and concepts of movement skills and movement knowledge; selfimage and personal development; and social development. They should also include descriptions of what units should look like when implemented in the classroom and how experiences within units are related to what is known about the particular level of development being addressed.

Suggestions for working with diverse groups of students should also be included in instructional resources. Strategies should be offered for helping students work together productively and managing technology-based media and materials so that appropriate resources are available when students need to use them. Support for the teacher should also include ways to connect the student's daily environment and experiences with classroom activities.

Ways to connect physical education with other areas of the curriculum should be given careful consideration in instructional resources for physical education teachers. Support for the teacher in carrying out assessment should include models for assessing student performance, helping students assess their own physical performance, and using assessment results.

Because parental and community involvement is a part of a wellplanned program, instructional resources should include suggestions for involving families and the community and keeping them informed about the program. Sample letters to family and community members about the value of the program, the rationale for what students are learning, and the instructional approaches being used might be included.

3

Guidelines for Teaching Physical Education

This chapter outlines the essential concepts, skills, and activities of a comprehensive physical education system for children in kindergarten through grade twelve. For each grade level the chapter presents the following elements:

— The primary emphasis of physical education for the grade level

— Background information on developmental appropriateness and readiness

— Actions and concepts to be highlighted in physical education instruction for each of the three goals of physical education

— Sample expectations for student performance.

The expectations for students should be based on the previous curriculum offered and the students' previous experiences, including those of students with disabilities. Although developmental appropriateness figures importantly in these guidelines, instructors should be aware that students are likely to display some characteristics and skills appropriate to groups above and below their age-mates. Instructors should also be aware of a general progression from learning the basics to being a self-directed learner that all students are capable of experiencing.

At the elementary level the physical education curriculum needs to focus on basic skills by having students participate in many types of ageappropriate activities. As their skills develop, students can begin to understand that correct practice will result in improved learning and development of competency. In the upper elementary grades, students can become involved in activities that will assist in their own learning and help them begin to appreciate individual differences in their peers.

At the middle school level, students can benefit from experiences that will assist them in evaluating and measuring their own performance. They can begin to recognize and develop practice schedules for different skills appropriate to their varying abilities. They can also be involved in activities in which they design schedules with and give appropriate feedback to their peers. Eventually, students can apply these concepts to new skills and thus transfer learning. At the high school level, students may design their own learning schedules based on their own choice of activities.

Throughout, it is important for planners and instructors to become aware of the total experience of a comprehensive system across age groups. Even during the early stages, a well-planned physical education program takes account of the long-term goals. Teachers of primary students are aware, for example, that students are moving toward the ultimate goal of making independent choices about physical activity in their teenage years. In addition, the element of pleasure in physical activity and an emphasis on pleasurable play should be a continual focus of physical education.

Kindergarten

Children at this stage are solo learners. They focus primarily on moving within space, including the general space around them and their own personal space. Nonlocomotor skills include how the body moves on its axis, and locomotor skills include moving in general space. Once the children are able to move effectively in their space, they focus on objects-for example, equipment, supplies, and materials. They also learn about and interpret their environment through play. They should move in a safe environment that helps them look forward to positive experiences in physical education.

Movement Skills and Movement Knowledge

At this stage children can be guided to move in their environment for the sheer enjoyment of exploring space and controlling their bodies. They learn basic movement skills, including creeping, crawling, walking, hopping, and galloping on the preferred foot, playing rhythmic games and song games, and participating in circle or partner walks and marches.

Nonlocomotor movement experiences include balancing, bending and stretching, twisting and turning, beating and shaking, tensing and relaxing, pushing and pulling, rising and falling, and participating in rhythmic and play activities that require those movements. Children in kindergarten also learn the concept of static stability by experiencing various balances that position the center of gravity over the base of support. They learn that the body is in a stable, balanced position when the center of gravity is directly over the base of support and that improvement occurs when a skill is practiced many times.

Object manipulation includes opportunities to manipulate and play with a wide variety of objects: lightweight balls, soft objects, beanbags, ribbons, hoops, and such student-made objects as sock balls, for example. At this stage students also perform free exploratory movement to rhythmic or musical accompaniment that is prerecorded or provided by the teacher or other students.

The kindergarten experience begins with the expansion of knowledge of the physical self through identification of body parts-both external (e.g., arms, legs, head, and facial features) and internal (e.g., heart and lungs). The kindergarten child's energy level and readiness to move contribute to a willingness to participate in aerobic-type activities. Through these activities students discover that the heart beats faster and breathing accelerates as they move their bodies. Learning about the importance of nutrition can begin at this level with instruction on selecting nutritious snack foods.

Self-Image and Personal Development

As kindergartners use their bodies to perform varied movements, they develop their own body image. Because self-image can be enhanced through movement experiences in physical education, children at this stage need many opportunities to experience personal feelings of success and achievement through movement.

Social Development

Basically ego-oriented, children in kindergarten tend to play alone in their own space. They are focused on themselves in the present. However, they also begin to recognize the concept of self and others; acknowledge that others may occupy their space; learn to move about in their space without interfering with others; and begin to learn to take turns and share in interaction with others. Children at this stage generally do not understand the purpose of rules but will follow rules delivered by adults.

Expectations

The student will be able to:

— Travel in different ways in a large group without bumping into others or falling.

— Balance while bending, twisting, or stretching.

— Strike a stationary ball with any part of the body.

— Identify various parts of the body and their location-for example, arms, legs, and hands.

— Recognize changes in heart rate.

— Follow adult-delivered rules.

Grade One

Students at this stage expand their movement skills to include qualities of space and time by learning to move in different directions at varying speeds. They explore a variety of movements, such as high-low and fast-slow. They also learn to recognize the element of time in movement -for example, how long it takes to move from one place to another and how long it takes an object to travel from one place to another.

Movement Skills and Movement Knowledge

Through movement experiences first graders develop an awareness of the concepts of space, time, and effort. These experiences should include many opportunities for children to feel the joy that results from having the ability and freedom to explore, discover, and express themselves through movement.

As they continue motor learning, first graders accept challenges to move through space with the added dimensions of time and effort, such as fast-slow and strong-weak. Direction in movement is introduced along with basic eye-hand and eye-foot manipulative skills. Locomotor activities include hopping on the nonpreferred foot; galloping on the nonpreferred foot; and marching, sliding, and performing other patterns according to specific rhythms. Nonlocomotor movements include symmetrical and asymmetrical balances, lifting and carrying, starting and stopping, swinging, swaying, curling, and stationary dodging.

Students make deliberate moves in specified directions. They learn the biomechanical principle of dynamic stability. That is, balance is inherent in all movement, and individuals can increase their static stability by widening their base of support and lowering their center of gravity. They also learn that movement begins when their center of gravity moves to the edge of their base of support, their center of gravity is raised, and their base of support is narrowed. For example, a student running, comes to a stop to maintain balance, and resumes running.

Students begin to manipulate objects with purposeful movement and learn to roll, toss underhand, bounce with two hands, retrieve, stationary-kick, and strike with the hand various objects that are safe and nonthreatening. Simple dances in columns and circles and basic partner dances are appropriate at this level.

Although the child's movement becomes more purposeful and performance more deliberate, the instructor should encourage interest in the performance of an activity rather than any particular level of achievement. Especially at the beginning of the year, the physical education program should include familiar and enjoyable games and activities that allow for each child's full participation.

First graders learn about the body's need for oxygen and food as fuel to supply the body with energy. They also learn about the role of the circulatory system in moving oxygenated blood to the muscles. They reflect on how their bodies feel as they experiment with different types of movement-for example, differing periods of time and types of space. The relationship of nutrition and exercise to physical strength and energy should be introduced at this level.

Self-Image and Personal Development

Children at this stage begin to form a personal body image through comparison with others. They learn that the body undergoes marked changes in height and weight and that those changes influence the movement and coordination of body parts.

Social Development

First graders participate in parallel play with other students and tend to be more involved in individual activities than in interaction with others. They continue to learn in groups but participate as individuals. Multicultural experiences should be interwoven as appropriate-beginning in grade one and continuing through each level.

Expectations

The student will be able to:

— Travel and change direction quickly in response to a signal.
— Travel in relationship to objects: over, under, behind, and through.
— Place the body and limbs in different positions, demonstrating high, middle, and low levels.
— Toss and catch a ball alone or with a partner.
— Learn to use equipment safely and responsibly.
— Begin to recognize changes in his or her body, such as changes in height and weight.
— Develop responsibility for expected behaviors on the playground and in the classroom.

Grade Two

At this stage students explore movement patterns with a partner to define movement in relation to another person, shape, or group. They learn by continuing to experience a variety of modalities, including kinesthetic learning. Since the students are highly flexible in interacting with partners, activities should encourage changes of partners. In the application of rules, fairness at this stage is flexible, and children are likely to make up their own rules as they play together.

Movement Skills and Movement Knowledge

Total physical response-response with the entire body-occurs in motor movement as the student learns to define movement in relation to another person, shape, group, or group shape. Locomotor patterns include leaping and skipping, dancing with a partner, and dancing in a double circle. Nonlocomotor movements include dynamic balancing, dodging while moving, pantomiming, and mirror moving. As students begin to play in partnerships, simple dances for couples, such as the Children's Polka, are appropriate. To understand movement and apply laws of motion at higher grade levels, students learn to describe movement and differentiate among speed, velocity, and acceleration. With partners second graders are able to compare various speeds and velocities. For example, students can talk about how fast they can run or walk and the difference between running and walking and other modes of locomotion.

Manipulative skills include catching a rolled ball; throwing and catching after one bounce (solo and with a partner); and kicking a stationary ball in a variety of ways. In addition to physical practice, students at this level should be encouraged to begin to use visualization and mental practice to reinforce learning. The study of exercise physiology considers how the heart and lungs work as partners in cardiorespiratory health. In pairs students monitor the pulse at rest, during exercise, and after exercise. As they participate in movement that accelerates breathing and pulse rate, they learn the concept of the body's need for exercise to accelerate breathing and pulse rates on a regular basis. Nutrition, with a focus on foods healthy for the heart, is another factor in developing students' knowledge and skills related to cardiorespiratory health.

Self-Image and Personal Development

Growth rates vary during this stage. As the children's awareness of others increases, they are able increasingly to see themselves in relation to others. They are also able to recognize and appreciate their own positive and negative feelings and those of others.

Social Development

In grade two children learn more about relationships between themselves and others. They move from the sense of self in isolation and begin to embrace the concept of we and partners. This is also a time when children's growing awareness of others can help to promote knowledge of individual differences and different cultures. That can be the springboard, in turn, for encouraging children to accept and appreciate differences in others.

The children are able to celebrate the successes of others and begin to recognize specific activities that contribute to feelings of joy and movement experiences that rely on cooperation. They consistently practice sharing and caring skills when playing with partners in movement activities and reinforce one another by giving and receiving encouragement.

Expectations

The student will be able to:

— Move backwards and change direction quickly and safely without falling.

— Jump and land, using a combination of one- and two-foot take-offs and landings.

— Throw a ball hard, demonstrating an overhand technique, a side orientation, and opposition.

— Jump a self-turned rope repeatedly.

— Skip, hop, gallop, and slide.

Grade Three

Reacting and responding to others take precedence at this stage. By now students have a self-image strong enough to tolerate differences in how others react to them and are better able to make well-defined combinations of movements. Groups should never number more than five, the number that provides everyone with many turns and allows for natural leaders and followers to emerge.

Movement Skills and Movement Knowledge

Students' motor ability increases as they gain greater control. They begin to develop a concept of the order of a sequence in movement and willingly experiment with and explore alternative movements. Third graders learn a variety of rhythmic patterns and gradeappropriate dances, using specific movement patterns, such as step-hop, step-swing, and two-step. Nonlocomotor skill development focuses on balance, including the use of apparatuses, inverted balances, balance on various body parts, and partner balances.

Students are able to describe muscular movement as the internal force that causes the body to change from a stationary to a moving object. They can also describe gravity, friction, and muscular movements as the external forces that cause the body to stop. They learn that specific types of movement provide benefits not only in developing skills but also in developing and maintaining health fitness. Striking skills, such as dribbling and volleying, continue to be refined.

Students are also able to discriminate among cues, adjust to cues, and determine appropriate movements for specific situations. This stage foreshadows the marked physical changes that will take place in later childhood. The exercise physiology experience for grade three includes an emphasis on the importance of aerobic exercise for cardiorespiratory health, including the principles of warming up before exercising and cooling down afterward. In keeping with the grade-level emphasis on continuity and change, students participate in warm-up exercises to change the body to a readiness state for more vigorous exercise. In extended periods of aerobic activity, they also experience continuity of effort in cardiorespiratory conditioning. A third healthfitness component, flexibility, is emphasized during the warm-up and cooling-down phases.

Self-Image and Personal Development

Third graders begin to express themselves by creating new movement patterns involving time, space, and flow. They continue to celebrate successes and identify activities contributing to feelings of joy through active play.

Social Development

Students learn through play to handle individual responsibilities and resolve personal differences, becoming more capable of working together for a common goal as they grow in their ability to cooperate and take turns. The teacher should encourage the formation of groups of mixed gender during structured sessions because at this level boys and girls tend to separate for free play. During this stage students begin to gain respect for other classmates and for the property of others, understand different types of play, and assist each other by practicing with a partner the rules of fair play. They learn to listen to each other and to react and respond appropriately.

Expectations

The student will be able to:

— Combine locomotor and nonlocomotor movements, such as combining various travel patterns in relation to music.

— Dribble a ball continuously, using the hands or feet to control it.

— Maintain flexibility by combining shapes, levels, and pathways into simple sequences.

— Recognize similar movement concepts in a variety of skills. For example, an underhand movement can be used in a variety of ways.

— Accept the feelings resulting from challenge, success, and failure in physical activity.

— Play and assist others in activities in groups of three to five.

GRADE FOUR

Fourth graders are at a stage between childhood and youth during which they are growing in definite patterns. Eye-hand coordination is improved, and fine-motor activities are becoming more skillful. In addition, the greatest gain in strength begins at this stage. Students have mastered many locomotor and nonlocomotor skills and are able to manipulate objects in a variety of ways. They can create a game, for example, when they are given an object and encouraged to play. Physiologically, while they are standing, their center of gravity is still located in the midsection of the body, making balance and manipulation of objects a challenge. Fourth graders are likely to test rules during play and challenge how rules apply to them. Further, they tend to regard rules as rigid and prescriptive. When exceptions to the rules have to be made, the logic and rationale of the rules should be emphasized.

Movement Skills and Movement Knowledge

In motor development students at this level are able to focus on refining their skills in comparison with proficiency standards. They begin to use space and distance appropriately as they progress toward accuracy in throwing, catching, manipulating the body in space, and striking with body parts and objects-for example, volleying and dribbling a basketball with the hands and moving a soccer ball with the feet. They also learn about the concepts of projection-for example, applying greater force to an object to make it travel farther and knowing how to generate force by maintaining firm contact with the ground when the object is released.

Rhythmic activities include specific dances that may be related to the history-social science curriculum, such as dances appropriate to specific regions, ethnic groups, and cultures. Students also learn that there are many ways to learn and practice movement skills and that a practice session can be conducted in a variety of ways. Whole practice involves learning an entire sequence of movements that combine into a complex skill pattern; partial practice involves concentrating on one fundamental movement. Some skills may be introduced whole, learned in parts, and then practiced whole. Fitness-conditioning activities focus on various types of health-fitness exercises and many ways to combine those exercises into an exercise program.

Another focus is on how physical exercise conditions the heart, lungs, and muscles. Students learn to differentiate between aerobic exercises that provide cardiorespiratory benefits and those that do not. They also learn about the importance of muscular endurance and strength as components of fitness. The role of nutrients in forming body composition and providing the energy needed to sustain physical movement should also be emphasized.

Self-Image and Personal Development

At this level students are ready to cope with success and failure and are more perceptive and accepting of similarities and differences. This is also a time for developing, in the individual and in the group, wholesome attitudes toward victory and defeat.

Appreciation of different styles of movement and the uniqueness of movement in various cultures begins to occur. Thus, fourth graders appreciate a sense of personal uniqueness in movement and become aware of the similarities and differences between themselves and others.

Social Development

Fourth graders are ready to take the initiative within the group and demonstrate leadership as well as learn to be a good follower. This level is appropriate for the introduction of more complex games that challenge and increase performance abilities and enhance social skills. Fourth graders are able to cooperate with a partner in using equipment and helping one another improve object manipulation skills.

Working together as part of large groups, they begin to appreciate personal differences and value the rights of others. They want to follow rules; thus, they need to learn to cope with conflicts and disputes by practicing conflict-resolution skills. While considering diversity in California, students observe that local demographics and geography influence the type of physical activities and recreational opportunities available within a given area-for example, skiing in the mountains and swimming and surfing at the ocean. Students also consider multicultural influences on the evolution of games and the varieties of game rules in different geographical areas.

Expectations

The student will be able to:

— Leap, leading with either foot.

— Hand-dribble and foot-dribble a ball while moving within a group.

— Jump and land for height and distance.

— Maintain continuous aerobic activity for a specified time.

— Describe healthful benefits that result from regular participation in physical activity.

— Recognize the fundamental strategies in simple games.

Grade Five

At this level students continue to manipulate a variety of objects according to more specific goals. Now accuracy and speed, with a focus on targets, become important. Eye-hand, eye-foot, and other forms of coordination begin to come together. Fifth graders try continually to improve their motor skills, celebrate their successes and achievements, and take pride in individual excellence. Groups are expanded to include more than five students, and cooperative learning parallels that of other academic subjects. At this level the concept of fairness is emphasized. Students may be willing to change rules in order to achieve fairness for all.

Movement Skills and Movement Knowledge

At this stage specific body types are more efficient in certain movements, skills, and activities as body size and strength increase steadily. As students continue to improve in motor performance, they become more proficient in basic skills, such as running, jumping, and throwing. The ten-year-old begins to concentrate on the development of selective motor skills.

Fifth-grade students manipulate objects through space with accuracy and with the added element of speed. As they practice for skill and accuracy, students learn that the desired expectation determines the type of practice needed to achieve that goal. One type of practice may be to concentrate on improving speed, another on improving accuracy, and still another on improving both.

In the application of Newton's second law, students experiment in throwing different sizes of balls (golf ball, shot, softball), discovering that smaller objects will travel farther than heavier objects when the same amount of force is used. When speed is the objective, they learn to use a flat trajectory. They learn that to catch an object, they must increase (1) the distance through which the object moves after contact; or (2) the size of the area that absorbs the force of the object.

In grade five students examine the role of the circulatory system and its relationship to overall health. They are taught to develop strength and flexibility, including the interaction of strength and flexibility with the ability to perform forceful movements or manipulate objects with force. Further, they are taught how to maintain a healthy body by balancing food intake with physical activity (calories consumed and calories expended) and regulating the ratio of lean to fat body tissue.

Self-Image and Personal Development

Students at this stage learn to establish goals and select the practice techniques appropriate to the most immediate goals. They play gamelike activities in which the use of more than two skills to achieve objectives in the game is emphasized. Experiencing individual satisfaction increases at this stage as a motivational factor for future participation in a variety of activities. Increasingly, fifth-graders are able to use the body in movement to communicate feelings and to appreciate the aesthetic aspects of physical performance and the pleasure of achieving goals they have set for themselves.

Social Development

Fifth graders thrive in small-group activity in which three to five students interact in cooperative play. They assume increasingly complex roles in cooperative activities; begin to develop an awareness of individual differences related to gender, cultural heritage, ethnicity, and physical ability; and appreciate the positive aspects of diversity. Social and game patterns include one against two, two against three, and two against two in activities such as goaltending. Students are beginning to recognize offensive and defensive play and understand that strategy is a skill to be developed within the context of play and games. Fifth graders know how to apply rules and demonstrate a sense of fairness in games and activities. Contemporary music and dance are popular. The California Raisin Dance and the Electric Slide, for example, can be modified to create more complex dance patterns.

Expectations

The student will be able to:

— Manipulate objects with accuracy and speed.

— Be involved in gamelike activities, with emphasis on more than two skills.

— Distinguish between compliance and noncompliance with game rules.
— Use fundamental strategies (i.e., offensive and defensive strategies) in simple games.
— Recognize that different body types are more effective in certain movement skills and activities.
— Begin to appreciate individual differences within small-group competition and cooperation.
— View the practice and perfection of performance in line and folk dances positively.

Grade Six

Students at this stage are able to combine various skills in cooperative activities and give appropriate feedback to others. More independent in thought and action than younger students, they are also more likely to seek out new challenges in individual and group activities. Despite their desire for independence, however, sixth graders are likely to be genuinely interested in helping others. Because their interest in team play and organized games is strong, learning experiences can focus on developing the skills required for cooperative effort toward a common goal.

Movement Skills and Movement Knowledge

Students at this level are ready to combine skills for practice in lead-up games (a team, individual, or dual activity leading to an organized sport). These activities facilitate the learning of physical skills while allowing for cooperative effort. A unit should be included in sixth grade on cooperative games that can be used as lead-up games for more traditional sports. Juggling, unicycling, pogo-stick activities, bowling, foot-bag skill games, and throwing activities add variety and challenge as students improve their eye-hand and eye-foot coordination. This is also an appropriate time to add tumbling to previously learned stunts. Students learn concepts related to Newton's third law. That is, when struck, an object will rebound in the opposite direction with the same amount of force with which it is hit. The harder an object is hit, the greater will be the force that causes the object to rebound in the opposite direction.

A child's development, which is influenced by heredity, hormones, nutrition, and exercise, is also influenced by cultural expectations and gender differences. Students should understand that the achievement of certain levels of physical skill is dependent on all of these factors and that they should accept individual differences.

Sixth graders are beginning to understand the purpose of each health-fitness component and the interrelatedness of all the fitness components in the development and maintenance of optimum health. Special emphasis should be given to the interaction of the circulatory and respiratory systems in conditioning for health fitness.

Self-Image and Personal Development

Students at this stage are able to recognize stylistic differences in performance, develop a more realistic self-image, and form collective attitudes as members of a group. They also begin to value looking good more than ever before as they become more aware of the varying levels of physical development within their peer group.

Despite the physiological differences that occur at this age, students are generally willing to work cooperatively toward a common goal because desire for recognition within the group is strong. The physical education experience should foster in each student a sense of acceptance and belonging and of being valued within the group or on a team.

Social Development

During lead-up games students at this level begin to recognize the validity of rule application and to accept that fairness applies to all. The grouping patterns for games can increase in size to six players. In keeping with the grade six history- social science focus on ancient civilizations, it is appropriate to introduce students to tribal dances and ethnic dances of contemporary or ancient cultures. Examples include the Pata Pata from South Africa, the Hora from Israel, and the High Life from Ghana.

As students work in cooperative groups, they learn to provide one another with feedback and support in skill execution. They learn through experimentation that specific, positive, corrective feedback improves skill development more rapidly than general, negative, or neutral feedback and that the more promptly feedback is given after performance, the more meaningful the feedback is.

Cooperation includes interacting with opponents in competitive activities to facilitate mutual development of skills. Sixth graders can accept and respect the performance of others, regardless of ability level, and are able to interact positively with others to develop friendships and participate in peer coaching activities with a partner.

Expectations

The student will be able to:

Throw a variety of objects, demonstrating both accuracy and distance (e.g., disklike objects, deck tennis rings, footballs). Design and play small group games that involve cooperating with others to keep an object away from opponents (basic offensive and defensive strategy-for example, by throwing, kicking, or dribbling a ball).

Design and refine a routine, combining various jump-rope movements to music, so that it can be repeated without error. Demonstrate correctly activities designed to improve and maintain muscular strength and endurance, flexibility, and cardiorespiratory functioning.

Participate in games, sports, dance, and outdoor pursuits, both in and outside of school, according to individual interests and capabilities. Recognize the role of games, sports, and dance in getting to know and understand people of diverse cultures.

Grade Seven

A well-planned physical education program takes into account the importance of the transition from sixth to eighth grade and the rapid physical, social, and emotional changes occurring at this level. Students are beginning to look for a sense of belonging, community, peer group, and team even as they are gaining more confidence in individual activities. They have an eagerness to test themselves, both individually and in groups. This is an appropriate time to introduce individual risk taking and individual sports rather than focus exclusively on team sports.

Movement Skills and Movement Knowledge

Students at this stage tend to enjoy risk-related activities. Unless the school curriculum provides such activities in a safe environment, the students are likely to pursue the activities on their own without supervision.

Appropriate activities include aquatics; combatives (e.g., self-defense and fencing); tumbling; gymnastics; individual and dual sports; and outdoor education, such as adventure-based activities and orienteering. Specific adventure-based activities might include problemsolving exercises in which students work in small groups to solve physical challenges; trust falls (the student falls backward into the arms of partners); low-rope activities, such as balancing on a log suspended above the ground; high-rope activities in which students are involved in rappelling or rock climbing; and rollerskating, skateboarding, and cycling. The tumbling unit introduced in grade six can be extended at this level to include apparatus for gymnastics and rhythmic gymnastics.

Seventh graders should learn more about the principles of spin and rebound. Spin results when force is applied off the center of an object. Students should become familiar with and begin to experiment with spins of various types: counterclockwise, clockwise, backspin, and topspin. They should learn how spin can be used to gain strategic advantage by players who understand how to apply it. Dance should include folk dances and other dances from cultures around the world to help students develop greater understanding and acceptance of their own heritage and that of others.

As for motor learning, students at this level should understand that performance is measurable in terms of technique, accuracy, distance, and speed. They should be able to chart their own motor skill development in specific activities and events.

Seventh graders are also able to understand the interrelationship of the health-fitness components in the development of optimum health and thus to select specific exercises for each component. This is an appropriate time to introduce the FIT guidelines for physical exercise, which are the appropriate frequency, intensity, and time required for benefits to be accrued in each health-fitness component. Students should learn the principles of overload, progression, and specificity in physical conditioning. Students' growth rates vary considerably during this period of development. Many experience their most rapid growth, and an increasing number show signs of puberty. All need to be aware that they must continue strenuous activity to maintain strength, speed, and endurance as their bodies change. They should study the impact of such factors as exercise, relaxation, nutrition, stress, and substance abuse on the body's ability to participate in physical exercise and on general well-being. Screening for posture deviation is required of all seventh graders, and parents must be notified when further examination is recommended.

Self-Image and Personal Development

The seventh grader is entering a time when he or she is more likely than ever before to take on new challenges, solve new problems, and be willing to take new risks. Risk taking involves new challenges and learning opportunities-trying out new equipment and new ways to use old equipment. Risk taking is attractive to students both alone and with others. They should be given a variety of opportunities to experience controlled risks through such activities as planned outdoor adventure activities and ropes courses. Students are also more likely to accept the challenge of setting personal goals for improvement related to health fitness and performance skills.

Social Development

Seventh graders are increasingly able to meet challenges, solve problems, and resolve conflicts within a group. They are more likely to express an appreciation for cooperation and fair play as they adhere to group rules. This is also a time when students develop confidence to overcome anxieties associated with attempting something new, making new friends, and beginning to accept their own limitations.

Expectations

The student will be able to:

— Leap, roll, balance, transfer weight, bat, volley, hand- and foot-dribble, and strike a ball with a paddle, using mature motor patterns.

— Participate in vigorous activity for a sustained period of time while maintaining a target heart rate.

— Identify proper warm-up, conditioning, and cooling-down techniques and the reasons for using them.

— Describe ways to use the body and movement activities to communicate ideas and feelings.

— Accept and respect the decisions made by game officials-whether they are students, teachers, or officials outside of school.
— Become engaged in activities that provide for challenge, problem solving, decision making, and risk taking.

Grade Eight

At this stage students are able to focus on a common group or team goal over the long term, working together to solve problems during group activities. The emphasis in physical education moves toward team sports, including defensive and offensive strategies. Students should be encouraged to continue participation in group activities because all aspects of the personal development of eighth graders, both physical and mental, are still evolving.

Movement Skills and Movement Knowledge

By the end of the eighth grade, students should have experienced a wide variety of activities. Now they can begin to see relationships among sports skills. For example, they may learn the underhand pitch for softball in one unit and transfer that skill to the underhand serve in volleyball and the serve in badminton. They should also be encouraged to understand that in certain situations transfer of learning can have a negative effect, such as learning the forehand drive in tennis and then applying it to the forehand drive in badminton.

A comparison of the offensive and defensive techniques used in team sports should be offered to help eighth graders learn the basic principles of strategy. In addition, students should have the opportunity to continue in a tumbling/gymnastics unit and a dance unit. Group dances, such as square, round, and contemporary line dances with directional changes requiring group cooperation, are appropriate. In eighth grade students learn the principles of rotation. That is, to rotate an object, one must apply torque. They also learn that the closer the mass is to the axis, the greater the rotary velocity will be. Eighth graders have many opportunities to experiment with these concepts, particularly during the gymnastics unit.

Students learn that growth in height and weight alters the mechanical nature of performance and that motor performance is related to all measures of maturity (chronological, anatomical, and physiological). Eighth graders are able to begin to design personal plans for a healthy life-style. Each student's plan should include exercises that take into account the FIT guidelines taught in grade seven and the principles of training. The importance of appropriate intensity in exercising should be emphasized as students learn to calculate their individual target heart rate for exercise and to understand the importance of cardiorespiratory conditioning. They should also be able to distinguish the health-related fitness components of cardiorespiratory endurance, muscular strength and endurance, flexibility, and body composition.

Self-Image and Personal Development

By eighth grade students should have developed skills needed to reduce stress. Their higher level of motor achievement provides a basis for establishing new personal goals that they can realistically attain.

Social Development

Students are able to accept responsibility for their behavior and resolve individual and group conflicts. They are mature enough to recognize the difference between ethical and unethical behavior and appreciate the importance of fair play, cooperation, and competition in team games, activities, and sports. They are also capable of playing on teams, making decisions, and solving problems associated with physical activities. Team games and team sports are of great interest and value to eighth graders of both genders because they help satisfy the students' need to feel a sense of belonging to a group.

The team-sports units should include the history, rules, and strategy of each sport. By this time students should understand that the rules are fair to all participants and allow for safe participation. They should also begin to generalize and understand that infringements of the rules involving other people are fouls; that infringements involving space, equipment, or time are violations; and that it is through the manipulation and understanding of the rules that strategies develop.

Group affiliation assumes added importance at this level, with emphasis being placed on team participation, roles of group members, group loyalty, and the identification of ethical and unethical behavior in group activities. Students begin to think of themselves as members of a team and learn to cooperate rather than dominate other team members in team and dual sports. They learn to identify and apply specific criteria for successful team participation and to lead and follow by sharing leadership positions.

Expectations

The student will be able to:

- Explore introductory outdoor skills (e.g., backpacking, hiking, boating, cycling, ropes courses).
- Perform a variety of simple folk, country, and creative dances.
- Practice appropriate ways of learning new skills or sports on his or her own.
- Improve and maintain appropriate body composition.
- Describe long-term physiological, psychological, and other benefits that may result from regular participation in physical activity.
- Recognize in playing team sports that rules are fair to all and allow for safe participation.
- Understand how growth in height and weight influences the mechanical nature of performance in physical activities.

Grade Nine

This is a stage at which students are able to synthesize much of what they have learned in the earlier grades, including knowledge of human growth, development, and physiology. Individuals are able to coalesce as a team and focus on the needs and contributions of other team members beyond themselves. Affiliation, a feeling of being connected and involved, is of primary importance to ninth graders. Students develop a willingness to acknowledge and respect stylistic differences in performance. The ninth-grade physical education program should encourage students to gain an appreciation of others' achievements, no matter how large or small, and to expand their ability to adapt to the needs of the group and demonstrate fairness toward all.

Movement Skills and Movement Knowledge

The major emphases of study in the ninth grade are fitness, team sports, gymnastics, and aquatics. In learning about fitness, the students become familiar with new concepts related to the physiology of exercise; become knowledgeable consumers in relation to fitness; and experience a wide variety of exercises for flexibility, muscular strength and endurance, and cardiorespiratory endurance. In team sports ninth graders should be encouraged to select a sport in which to specialize; learn the history, rules, and strategies of the sport; and become proficient in the appropriate skills. The gymnastics unit should be an extension of the earlier tumbling and gymnastics classes. Here, too, students should be encouraged to select an event in which to specialize. For those students who already demonstrate proficiency in swimming, classes in water polo, skin diving, or advanced swimming can be offered. During an aquatics unit the students should learn the biomechanical principle of buoyancy. That is, to move efficiently through water, they must streamline their bodies to reduce the effect of drag. In addition, the swimmer's size, shape, surface, and speed of movement are factors affecting performance in swimming.

In grade nine the student is expected to develop an in-depth understanding of the components of total health fitness in a unit that empha-sizes the physiological, psychological, and social benefits of a healthy, active life-style.

Students should also begin to identify preferences for types of physical activity that can be pursued over the long term for fitness and recreation, including individual, dual, or team sports. Ninth graders should be able to explain the social, personal, and health benefits of developing skills in sports, games, and dance. They should be able to describe the aesthetic qualities of movement; feel good as they move efficiently and effectively; and develop the ability to evaluate personal needs, interests, and capacities that contribute to their movement choices.

Self-Image and Personal Development

In physical education experiences the ninth grader should demonstrate patterns of behavior that reflect sound mental and emotional health, positive self-image, and acceptance of the total self. To help students achieve self-realization through physical activity, the physical education instructor should guide the student's choice of fitness programs and activities to ensure a healthy life-style throughout life. Each student should set personal goals for health and fitness, including goals for improving health through physical exercise.

Social Development

Ninth graders have the capacity to demonstrate mature teamwork by successfully resolving conflicts within the group. They should learn to cooperate in teamwork and in competition, analyze situations, find solutions to problems, obey rules, work for delayed rewards, and persevere toward a goal. The ninth grader is becoming increasingly more interested in sports as both participant and spectator. This increased interest is associated with several factors in addition to physical conditioning. For example, students have more choices in transportation and consumer spending. And they are bombarded with advertisements for all types of participant and spectator sports.

Expectations

The student will be able to:

— Analyze offensive and defensive strategies in games and sports.

— Participate in an individualized fitness program.

— Identify and follow rules while playing sports and games.

— Identify ways in which rules are more alike than different and describe the difference between violations and fouls.

GRADE TEN

Students at this stage are capable of choosing the physical activities they want to pursue. They are more able to generalize from previous experiences and to apply biomechanical principles to the analysis of a variety of movement skills. A well-planned physical education program will offer students a wide variety of opportunities. It will focus on individual or team sports of choice, dance, and personal defense, among other activities.

Movement Skills and Movement Knowledge

The five emphases of study for the tenth grade are individual and dual sports, outdoor education, combatives, dance, and analysis of movement. The individual or dual sport may be of the student's own choosing and may include such outdoor activities as orienteering, rock climbing, backpacking, and skiing. A personal defense class meets the combatives requirement and teaches students to avoid dangerous situations while preparing to defend themselves. The dance unit can be an extension of units taught at earlier grade levels. It can also be an elective that allows students to specialize in a specific type of dance at an intermediate or advanced level.

The analysis-of-movement class should conclude grade ten whenever possible. Reviewing what they have learned throughout the kindergarten through grade ten physical education curriculum, students should explore the reasons for physical education being taught in school, including the relationship between physical education and personal and social development. This class should also prepare students to be informed consumers in physical and recreational activities they plan to pursue outside of school. By the end of this unit, students should have developed a lifetime plan for physical fitness and activity. At this grade level students demonstrate improved performance, in part because their perceptual feedback has improved. They have acquired skills that are basic to efficient movement. In addition, they should have acquired a high level of physical fitness. They should be able to analyze the physiological and mechanical principles involved in human movement and make adjustments in physical exercise to achieve personal goals for fitness or motor performance or both.

The application of the principles of levers to movement should be introduced in tenth grade. The human skeletal system is made up primarily of third-class levers. Because the force arm (muscle) for human beings cannot be lengthened, the students should learn that in order to increase the force at impact with an object, they must strengthen the muscle or lengthen the striking element to increase the force. Students can apply these concepts in activities such as golf (by using a longer shaft when driving) and tennis (by straightening the arm at the moment of impact in the serve).

Self-Image and Personal Development

The awareness tenth graders have of the importance of commitment and dedication in physical education contributes to their desire to pursue excellence in a variety of ways-socially, emotionally, and intellectually. The tenth-grade physical education curriculum should emphasize that while learning any new skill, individuals go through three stages of learning: (1) the cognitive phase; (2) the practice phase; and (3) the automatic phase, in which skills can be performed without concentrated attention. Although moving through this cycle takes time, students at the high school level are mature enough to reach the automatic phase in selected skills.

Tenth-grade students should be encouraged to evaluate the potential benefits and risks of available exercise programs in the school and the community and the cost-effectiveness of exercise programs offered to students as consumers. Each student should plan a personal exercise program that is physiologically sound and appropriate to his or her needs, interests, level of ability, and goals for health fitness.

Social Development

Tenth graders are often ready to assume leadership roles. By serving as peer coaches, they can take the initiative to assist other students by analyzing their application of the principles of biomechanics and by providing feedback and suggestions for improvement. As they become more concerned with social etiquette, they can study the ways in which society's rules are expressed through games and sports. In addition, they can develop an awareness of the ways in which society influences their choice of lifestyle as to types of physical activity and the degree of their participation in physical activity in and out of school. Students at this level also develop an appreciation of movement as an art form that reflects cultural values.

Expectations

The student will be able to:

— Demonstrate basic competence in physical activities selected from each of the following categories: aquatics; self-defense; dance; individual, dual, and team activities and sports; and outdoor pursuits.

— Perform a variety of dances (folk, country, social, and creative) with fluency and in time to accompaniment.

— Use biomechanical concepts and principles to analyze and improve performance of self and others.

— Discuss the importance of balanced nutrition for a maintaining a healthy life-style.

— Design and implement a personal fitness program that relates to total wellness.

— Participate in a variety of game, sport, and dance activities representing different cultural backgrounds.

— Discuss the historical roles of games, sports, and dance in the cultural life of a population.

— Acknowledge and respect stylistic differences in performance.

Grades and Eleven and Twelve

Students at this level continue to specialize in activities of their own choosing. In addition, they can pursue excellence in the activities they choose, following a specific regimen and honing specific skills. They are able to develop a personalized plan for lifetime fitness by assessing personal needs, interests, abilities, and opportunities in the area of fitness and by selecting activities that contribute to the achievement of personal fitness goals. They can also focus on combatives; outdoor education; aquatics; team sports and individual and dual sports of choice; tumbling; gymnastics; and dance.

They can apply knowledge, skills, and attitudes acquired in physical education experiences from kindergarten through grade twelve to become proficient in one or more activities that lead to achieving personal goals for lifetime fitness. Schools should be encouraged to be creative in developing their physical education electives for these grade levels.

Movement Skills and Movement Knowledge

By the eleventh and twelfth grades, students are prepared to focus on the activities they plan to pursue after graduation from high school. They are able to explain why an individual's pursuit of excellence in any arena is an evolving process requiring commitment, courage, confidence, initiative, and perseverance. They have learned that self-expression through physical activity is of great value in developing and maintaining the healthy mind and body needed to excel in life. Students should be encouraged to select a variety of activities that correspond to their personal needs, interests, and capacities. They should also be encouraged to reassess their changing needs and interests continually as they grow and mature. Students should be encouraged to select activities in which they will continue to specialize. Therefore, the biomechanical principles they study should be directly related to the activities they select. The students should also be encouraged to apply their knowledge of exercise physiology in planning and pursuing life-styles conducive to maintaining optimum health.

Self-Image and Personal Development

The senior high school student is at a stage where he or she can develop an increased interest in selecting activities in accordance with personal body type and capacities. By the eleventh grade students should have learned to evaluate personal performance in a variety of activities. They should be given the opportunity for self-direction in the selection of activities that can be enjoyed for health and fitness throughout life. Having selected activities for specialization, the student should have the motivation to learn. Students should be aware that the learning process takes them through three stages of learning and should understand that they must repeat and practice skills in a variety of ways in order to achieve excellence. They should also know how to measure their performance at different stages to maintain their motivation and adjust their goals for future training.

By the eleventh and twelfth grades, students are prepared to focus on the activities they plan to pursue for recreation or a career after graduation from high school. Elective units in a wide range of activities should last for a sufficient period of time. Students who complete these classes should be well prepared to continue the activity on their own.

Social Development

Students should be encouraged to work in small groups to provide one another with specific positive/corrective feedback so that individual excellence can be achieved. They should apply social skills acquired in physical education activities in preschool through grade twelve to enhance their own experience and the experience of others with whom they are involved in physical and social activities. They should also be encouraged to support and participate in community organizations that promote health and fitness by providing lifelong recreational opportunities for people of all ages.

Expectations

The student will be able to:

Grade eleven:

— Use the principles of movement to accomplish a task with the least effort.

— Demonstrate some mastery of skills in games, sports, and dances and participate in intramural programs.

— Comprehend the correct elements of various movements, strategies, safety procedures, and basic rules.

— Show evidence of developing and maintaining physical fitness to achieve the goal of a healthy life-style.

— Show evidence of a positive self-image.

— Share in the responsibility of group action and problem solving as a member of a group or team.

Grade twelve:

— Excel and continue in an activity of choice, such as a sport, dance, gymnastics, or aquatics.
— Demonstrate advanced competence in at least one activity from the curriculum.
— Be able to design and execute a physical fitness program, recognizing that changes in life-style may progress over time from vigorous activities to mild exercise, including walking.
— Accept the ways in which personal characteristics, performance styles, and activity preferences will change over the life cycle.
— Know about career opportunities in physical education and related fields.
— Evaluate critically the claims made in advertisements about commercial products and programs.

Environment Needed for a Quality Programme Physical Education

A positive, supportive environment is important to the success of the overall physical education program. Support for physical education should include the following elements:

— Physical education is recognized as an integral part of the school curriculum. Physical education continually supports and interacts with other subject areas.
— Physical education is included as part of a planned staff development program.
— Facilities, equipment, and supplies are provided that are safe and adequate.
— The psychological environment enables and encourages all students succeed in physical education.
— The physical education program involves the school, the home, and the community.

Integral Part of the School Curriculum

As an integral part of the school curriculum, physical education should be taught by qualified professionals who have been trained in physical education or who have participated in a program of professional development focusing on the teaching of physical education. Classes for children and youths with special needs or disabilities should be taught by physical education teachers who know how to design and implement programs for such students. A quality physical education program provides equal access for all students and guarantees opportunities for maximum participation, optimum development, and appropriate indi-vidual attention. Opportunities for personal attention, individualized instruction, and time on task should be included. Physical education teachers should be encouraged to participate on school or district interdisciplinary teams to develop the physical education curriculum. In a well-planned program the physical education teacher assumes responsibility for

(1) implementing the physical education curriculum;

(2) relating physical education to other subject areas;

(3) working with other professionals to create interdisciplinary approaches to learning; and

(4) promoting the cooperation of school, home, and community in providing the highest-quality physical education experience possible for every student.

Integration with Other Subject Areas

Physical education should continually support and interact with the other subject areas. For example, in its emphasis on personal health and the need for a healthy life-style, physical education reinforces but does not supplant health education. Teachers of physical education and health education should work together to integrate their curricula to reinforce the importance of maintaining an active and healthy life-style.

Both can emphasize skills related to refusing negative pressures and influences, resolving conflicts, and coping with pressure, all of which are necessary for positive social interaction and healthy development. Physical education classes provide a natural environment for the development of personal and social skills transferable to other situations and learning in other subject areas. There is a natural correlation, for example, between cooperative learning activities related to understanding the place of rules and strategies in physical education and the teaching of civic values, rights, and responsibilities in history-social science.

Continual interaction should occur between teachers of physical education and the rest of the staff. Through this interaction physical education and the other disciplines support and reinforce one other. Other examples of integration with the rest of the curriculum include the following:

— Natural sciences-through concepts related to gravity, levers, motion, physics, anatomy, biomechanics, and exercise physiology
— Home economics-through the study of exercise physiology and nutrition
— History-social science-through an emphasis on guiding students to become active, productive members of a democratic society; work cooperatively in groups and teams; and develop an understanding of others through cross-cultural and multicultural games, dances, and other activities
— English-language arts-through applying physical education experiences in written assignments and other activities requiring communication skills
— Mathematics-through recording results and calculating probabilities, percentages, and averages related to physical activity or creating graphs to demonstrate measurements and comparisons of personal progress

— Visual and performing arts-through a shared emphasis on aesthetic perception, creative expression, rhythm, tempo, and meter

— Career-vocational education-through the study of careers in such areas as teaching, recreation, health, fitness, dance performance, and sports broadcasting

Physical education includes more than the education of the physical body. All subject areas should function as integrated components in the education of the total individual.

Planned Staff Development Program

A variety of staff development activities should be available to enhance the physical education program. Teachers of physical education should be encouraged to

(1) participate in ongoing staff development to improve instructional strategies and program implementation;

(2) remain current on educational research;

(3) learn to be effective with an increasingly diverse student population; and

(4) enjoy the benefits of working and learning with other professionals in the field.

They should also be encouraged to work with local colleges or universities to influence preservice training and provide in-service training opportunities. At the school level physical education teachers should have opportunities to meet regularly with each other and with members of other departments or grade levels to assess the effectiveness of programs and plan revisions. Ensuring compliance with state and federal mandates should be an important part of the assessment process as well. Teachers should be encouraged to become involved in professional organizations and contribute their expertise to staff development projects in physical education at the local, state, and national levels.

Adequate Facilities, Equipment, and Supplies

Indoor and outdoor facilities must be sufficient in number, appropriate to the needs of all students, and accessible to the disabled. Dressing rooms must be clean and safe, adequate for the number of students served, and appropriately supervised without requiring physical education instructors to lose instructional time because of supervision. Equipment and supplies should be sufficient in quantity and quality to provide all students with opportunities to enjoy maximum participation. Safety is an important priority in the environment for a quality physical education program. Staff members must be aware of safety concerns, protect students from unsafe equipment or facilities, and expect students to ensure their own safety and that of others. A student's lack of proficiency in English should not influence this priority in any way. Provisions should be made to ensure that all limited-Englishproficient students understand rules and expectations regarding safety. Others to be considered in ensuring the safety of all students should be persons with disabilities.

Appropriate Psychological Environment

An appropriate environment for a quality physical education program enables and encourages all students to discover new concepts, skills, and abilities through movement experiences and other aspects of the physical education program. The atmosphere should be a nonthreatening one in which every student feels that to risk trying something new is safe physically, emotionally, and socially. Emphasis should be placed throughout on the development of movement skills, fitness and wellness, self-confidence, and social skills.

Because of the complexities of human growth and development and individual and cultural differences among students, a comprehensive physical education program should include a wide variety of movement experiences and teaching-learning strategies. All students should have the opportunity to be successful. Throughout, the student must experience a climate of respect-for oneself, for others, and for physical education generally, especially when students are being directed in attempts to refine skills or are being disciplined. Disciplinary procedures should be appropriate to the infraction, and the assignment of physical exercise should not be used as punishment. To do so will not instill in the student a love of physical activity.

Another important aspect of the psychological environment is an emphasis on accepting and celebrating ethnic and cultural diversity, one of the most challenging issues in education. Physical education offers unique opportunities to bring students together in nonthreatening ways that emphasize fairness and cooperation. Because physical education involves students in working and playing together, students must be taught the personal and social skills, values, and attitudes needed for effective, positive social interaction. Disparaging remarks about an individual's disabilities, ethnicity, gender, native language, race, religion, or sexual orientation should not be tolerated.

The physical education program must comply fully with all federal and state mandates. Appropriate instruction in physical education for culturally diverse populations may require special teaching skills and a focus on students' unique needs. Teachers must avoid cultural or gender biases and refrain from stereotyping students. Students from different cultures may respond differently to directions from the teacher, praise and acknowledgment from others, perceived expectations, and physical interaction. Teachers should learn to recognize and understand the influence of their students' cultural heritage and learn to accommodate diversity while achieving the goals of the physical education curriculum.

Cooperation of School, Home, and Community

Although the school is the primary learning environment for physical education, the home and community also play significant roles. Only through the cooperation of the school, the home, and the community can students become fully prepared for lifelong participation in physical activity and effective social interaction. The school site can become a focus for cooperation among families and outside support systems. Designating the school as the contact point provides families with more opportunities to receive services that benefit the child's health and development. For example, interaction of school and family can help to promote an acceptance of physically active and healthier, happier, more productive life-styles throughout the community.

Schools can establish centers for wellness that provide assessment of physical well-being, individual counseling, and a variety of fitness activities. They can also involve families in other extracurricular activities at the school site and coordinate school and community recreational programs. The community, working closely with the school, can play an active role in promoting fitness and wellness by providing opportunities for physical activity for families and individuals. Through participation in a variety of physical activities at school, students will be better prepared to take advantage of opportunities for physical activity provided in the home or in the community.

4

Socio-constructive Approach to PE Teacher Training

In physical education, three dominant discourses in teacher training exist, namely pedagogy of performance, critical pedagogy and postmodern pedagogy. The pedagogy of performance is traditional pedagogy. It finds its essence in techniques and strategies of practical application. It mostly involves questions which tend towards probable results. This paradigm is called scientific or positivist. According to the critical pedagogy in physical education, the most appropriate discourse in teacher training programs is not the scientific one, but rather the one claiming social justice. The key concepts which constitute the foundations of this paradigm are liberation, dialogue, criticism and practice.

Critical pedagogy puts an emphasis on fields related to ethics, morals and politics. Its aim is to relate diverse elements such as school, physical education, teachers and the social reality. The heart of critical pedagogy is found in history. And it is through critical reflection about history that it trains teachers who reflect about their daily practice and about the political, social and moral dimensions of their educative acts.

Postmodern pedagogy is associated with the critical paradigm, in the sense that they both question the positivist foundations. Nevertheless, it denies the neomarxist discourse of critical pedagogy. It also rejects the importance that critical pedagogy gives to rationality and prefers the search for intersubjective truth which finds its essence in the multiplicity of interpretations. The aims of postmodern pedagogy is to be a significant answer to the social, cultural and economic conditions which characterize contemporary capitalism.

In a study concerning the different approaches in teacher training in physical education, Kirk advocates that it is the paradigm of performance that is most popular that is, a dualistic pedagogy, which tends to isolate the two dimensions of learning, namely theory and practice. According to Kirk, the consequences are negative, for this conception of education forms prospective teachers who are somewhat or not at all autonomous, critical or conscious of their political and moral role within their profession. Moreover, as Kirk mentions, these prospective teachers are not trained to create relationships by themselves. As a consequence, within the reality of daily practice, they are bewildered and incapable of dealing adequately with classroom problems when they happen.

It is believed that most teacher training programs produce somewhat passive and docile 'transmitters' of information rather than 'creators' conscious of the importance of their role. According to the supporters of critical and postmodern pedagogies, the teacher training programs at most universities still consider knowledge as an objective notion, which 'exists somewhere', waiting to be discovered and learned.

Knowledge is thus not intended to provoke reflection and questioning amongst prospective teachers, but merely to be memorized. The impact of this static training on the education of youngsters can be problematic. Indeed, the teacher who has not developed the habit of thinking in a critical, autonomous and responsible fashion will not create, in her or his classroom, a culture of critical reflection and moral behavior. As a consequence, there is little chance that future generations will develop such a culture.

The problems in physical education teacher training programs seem to have two sources:

1. the theoretical and practical dimensions of teaching are isolated one from the other, and do not respect the fundamental principle of continuity.

2. the training given to prospective teachers increases the standing of memorization and comprehension, instead of the development of higher order thinking skills such as autonomous, critical and responsible thinking.

CONSTRUCTIVISM

Constructivism is an epistemology about the search for and construction of personal interpretation and understanding in an age of ready-made knowledge.

Giambasttista Vico was a professor of rhetoric at the University of Naples. He was first influenced by Cartesian epistemology, but he soon criticized its dualism. Vico complained that Descartes arrived at a mechanistic view of human nature, which he considered faulty. For him, a person is not merely someone who reasons from self-evident principles; feelings must also be taken into account along with the individual's creativity. Vico viewed education as an essentially moral enterprise. Indeed, for him, a human being is an active totality, developing her or his own history. Also, he insisted that education ought not to be concerned merely with empty erudition, but with the development of language, which supposes a moral dimension.

Vico appears as one of the first philosophers offering to the world of education a monist epistemology, which breaks with the traditional conception of knowledge. He was the first one to assert that knowledge does not exist 'out there' with a life of its own, and to support the constructivist activity of human reason. Moreover, Vico laid another stone in the development of a new conception of academic research, when he claimed that not all subjects should be determined by the same method, and thus, that the mathematical method should not be appropriate for the humanities. Vico opened the door to qualitative research which is more concerned with dialogue and uncertainty.

In the nineteenth century and at the beginning of the twentieth century, pragmatists and particularly instrumentalists contributed to the development of the constructivist conception. Then, in the twentieth century, Jean Piaget gave it an explicit life. Piaget is the major figure in constructivism, breaking with conventional ideas concerning the acquisition of knowledge related to Vico's ideas. Piaget's conception of learning and knowing leads to a constructivist epistemology, which is in opposition to traditional ones, by which knowledge should or could represent reality.

In Western history, most philosophers tried to find answers to the following epistemological questions: 'What is knowledge?' 'Does certainty exist?' Piaget, on the contrary, wondered 'How can a child reach what we call knowledge?' This means that Piaget, instead of considering that knowledge represents a real world that exists independently of the individual's experience, considered that knowledge is a tool that contributes to adaptation. When we use the word 'adaptation', here, we refer to two levels: biological and conceptual.

In constructivism, rational knowledge always concerns the field of experiences and abstractions that have been constructed by the individual. The construction of paradigms by the individual is based on the belief that coming experiences will be similar to past experiences. 'Experience', here, does not mean everything that reaches consciousness. It consists mainly of sensations and empirical and reflective abstractions that we are aware of. In this sense, experience is essentially and completely subjective.

Scientific knowledge is not omnipotent nor does it reflect a set of fixed objective laws, for it is a social construction. In this perspective, a scientific paradigm is never considered as the only possibility for solving problems. Furthermore, constructivism does not search for 'truth', but for theoretical paradigms that have shown their viability within their field of experience and compatibility with other paradigms. In other words, scientific paradigms carry the status of means and not ends. Also, constructivism does not consider that language is a tool to 'transport' information, knowledge and ideas from one person (knower) to another (learner).

The last point noted by von Glasersfeld about language introduces the notion of activity and responsibility in education, for it supposes that language must be conceived as one of the tools to guide the students in their reflexive process which consists in the organization of the representations formed by the taught knowledge. The distinction between students as discoverers or inventors is thus assumed. If students are discoverers, they look at the world through the 'keyhole'; if they are inventors, they participate in an enterprise where they continuously invent the rules, norms and traditions. In socioconstructivism, students are considered as living organisms who create a theory of the world.

The actual act of teaching is permeated with a conception of learning that results from a script which was written 2500 years ago and that can be summarized in these terms: the observer and the objects observed are two independent and separate entities; it is the cognitive ability of the learner that can relate these two elements; as a result, there is knowledge or, more explicitly, knowledge about objective reality which stands 'out there', waiting to be discovered. This promotes the learner's cognitive passivity, for she or he is not an active subject who constructs her or his system of comprehension, but a receptacle that receives the predigested heritage of previous generations. Constructivism, however, refuses to separate the 'subject who searches for knowledge' and the 'things to know' and to consider them as two distinct entities.

Traditional teaching transmits a conception of a static and never-changing world and leads the learners to believe that objective knowledge that is presented to them describes a unique 'reality'. In this context, teaching is characterized by the transmission of isolated bits of knowledge, the use of predictive testing, and the measuring of performance on out-of-context tasks. Traditional teaching is sometimes called positivism or objectivism; others would call it educational reductionism.

While studying conceptual development that is, the conditions that favor evolution in students' cognitive structure, some researchers propose the importance of social interactions in the construction of knowledge. They considered that peers are essential in the development of one's concepts and perspectives, for an individual will hardly revise her or his personal interpretation and perspective unless she or he is confronted with others' questions, doubts, and criticisms. From Vygotsky's perspective, for example, the socioconstructivist epistemology puts a special emphasis on the role of social interactions in the development of the person.

In this epistemology, the key point is the notion of 'conflict', namely a structured conflict, which causes cognitive changes and progress. This conflict is possible when interactions occur and favor the simultaneous expression of a diversity of actions, solutions and discourses. It is diversity itself which provokes a cognitive conflict in the listener which drives her or him to enter into a reflective process. Indeed, on many occasions, work in interaction reveals a difference in the responses. This difference is due to the participants' different focuses or points of view. As a result, there is a disequilibrium which comes from the awareness of another possible good answer.

Some authors observed that the impact of opposed responses is more significant when these are accompanied by verbal argumentations. At the same time, they realized the poor quality of the latter. Although socioconstructivism arose from Piagetian structuralism, it is fundamentally different from Piaget's perspective, which considers that social interactions and transmissions cannot, by themselves, explain the child's development and learning. For instance, Piaget explained that the logical structure developed by the individual contributes more to children's moral development than do social consensus, social conventions or the rules of the group. Actually, the characteristic of the Piagetian conception of conflict is more psychological than social: a conflict results from confrontations and contradictions within the individual's actions or anticipations. We could say that the nature of conflict, for Piaget, is 'infra-individual' and not 'inter-individual' as Doise, Mugny and Perret-Clermont explicitly contend.

In short, the main characteristics of constructivism, which is a theory about the formation of knowledge and not about human beings, are the following:

1) knowledge cannot be transmitted from one person to another person, but is always constructed and contingent.
2) Cognition has to be seen as an adaptive function which is used to organize the world around us, rather than to discover reality.

Regarding socioconstructivism, we could say that: the developmental process happens by means of questioning and cognitive conflicts; personal evolution is promoted by social interactions; a school's first aim is to develop autonomous and critical subjects and not standardized students.

Philosophy for Children Pedagogy

Matthew Lipman and Ann Margaret Sharp conceived a program of philosophy for children, in the 1970's. This program postulates that young students can develop their higher order thinking skills inasmuch as school creates the conditions that favor dialogue among peers. We find some interesting relationships between the socioconstructivist epistemology and the Philosophy for children pedagogy. The latter considers that too many societies still function according to a hierarchical model, and that children, like women, blacks and the poor, are marginalized and are not respected. Too often, they are treated as objects in the sense that they are considered incapable of investigating their own social reality. In this sense, it meets the socioconstructivist objection.

Philosophy for children and socioconstructivism consider it essential to give all persons a locus to think and to construct their own interpretation and representation of the world. Both consider that education should give the marginalized a voice in articulating their perception of their problems and relevant solutions.

Like the Philosophy for children pedagogy, socio-constructivism represents an alternative view of society. Both are opposed to the traditional and dominant discourse, and in its own terms, advocates the creation of more just and equitable systems, emancipation, autonomy and critical knowledge. Finally, they both propose an alternative form of knowing which could be called, after Maguire, 'interpretive knowledge'.

Interpretive knowledge stresses the importance of understanding how human interactions function, in order to create the conditions for cooperation and emancipation. It considers that 'objectivity is an illusion because it suggests that it is possible to separate the subject of knowledge, the knower, from the object, the known'.

Philosophy for children and socioconstructivism call for individual and collective action. Actually, they search for and attempt to develop meanings within a community of peers, in order to create a more just and significant reality. It assumes critical knowledge that is, a dialectical relationship between reflection and action or between theory and practice.

To use the metaphor of the old man in Carl's story, we could say that Philosophy for children and constructivist (or socioconstructivist) paradigm represent some of the ways for the self and the collectivity to start the active search for the sacred ground of his or their own thinking, acting and being. Technological systems and pedagogies based upon performance sell the illusion of education as a spectacle in which beings exchange their own selves for an appearance, as though these were the 'necessary steps' to be taken and to promote in order to 'get better'.

For instance, in Quebec, in the field of physical education, although all models of intervention do not come from a traditional epistemology, sociocon-structivism is valued not at all or very little in the teacher training programs. Some marginalized scholars appear, however, to be going in this direction. For instance, since 1981, Arthur Sheedy has condemned the technicist approach. He notes that the regular use of such a paradigm creates a distance between the body and the self, in the sense that it promotes the students in physical education to acquire scientific knowledge and to develop techniques of gestures in ways that require the separation of thought and feeling. Sheedy is aware that this reductionist approach reflects the culture in which it evolves.

From another intellectual tradition, but with the same desire for radical change, the Confederation des educateurs et educatrices physiques du Quebec (CEEPQ) claims that physical education must change its perspective, forget about the development of the mere biological machine, and favor the development of all dimensions of the person.

Also, Frangois Desbiens calls for 'transdisciplinarity', a training model whose goal is to integrate theory and practice and in which autonomous and critical thinking is valued. This model gives rise to the organization, planning and evaluation of the apprenticeship by the self. In the United States and around the world, the situation seems to be similar to the one in Quebec. Some studies condemn the fact that reflection about the social, moral and political aspects of teaching are missing from prospective teachers' training. Scholars in physical education point to the detrimental influence of the technicist perspective and promote the development of 'reflective practitioners', to use Schon's denomination.

However, according to Tsangaridou and O'Sullivan, despite the emphasis on reflection in teacher education theories, empirical work on reflective teaching to support these propositions is in its infancy. Actually, a review of the literature shows not much more than the empirical studies of Gore, Sebren, Rovegno and Tsangaridou and O'Sullivan. The investigation of Tsangaridou and O'Sullivan, for instance, reached three major conclusions.

First, evidence from their study indicated that reflective pedagogical strategies such as logs, video commentaries and school observations influenced prospective teachers to develop more analytical responses to their teaching in physical education, and that 'pedagogical reflective strategies that included more challenging questions influenced the level of reflection of the preservice teachers.'

Second, it showed that the prospective teachers place asymmetrical emphasis on the foci of reflection, since the focus of reflection was mostly dominated by the technical issues of teaching (reflecting on instructional or managerial aspects of teaching) as distinct from situational (reflecting on contextual aspects of teaching) and sensitizing (reflecting on social, moral, ethical or political aspects of teaching) issues.

Third, Tsangaridou and O'Sullivan concluded that supervisors should also receive theoretical and practical knowledge on ways to enhance prospective teachers' reflective abilities, that they should know how to use dialogue in supervisory conferences in ways that challenge preservice teachers to think and reflect about different aspects of teaching and schooling. In the present study, it was the participants who suggested that their supervisors ask them questions to help them think and analyze their teaching.

Alternative Approach

The essence of the alternative approach that we propose in teacher training in physical education is grounded epistemologically in socioconstructivism. Along with Giroux and Simon's claim, we claim that: "We are not concerned with simply motivating students to learn, but rather establishing the conditions of learning that enable them to locate tbemselves in society and to interrogate the adequacy of that location as both a pedagogical and political question." In this sense, the aims of the alternative approach that we propose are the following:

l) to enable prospective teachers to think in an autonomous, critical and responsible fashion and, in so doing, make them aware of the importance of their role in the education of young generations;

2) to help them unify the theoretical and practical dimensions of their training in physical education and, in so doing, help them transfer the knowledge to educative practice in order to solve properly the problems they will encounter.

As professors involved in teacher training, we are mainly concerned about the integration of theory and practice, since we agree that 'theoretical and practical knowledge are inextricably interlinked in any complex action or series of actions such as teaching.' Also, we believe that it is the dialectical relationship between theory and practice that creates cognitive conflicts in the students' minds, and therefore, leads to significant education. Traditional dogmatic teaching cannot, by itself, meaningfully educate prospective teachers in physical education. Nor can reflexion alone about students' personal experience result in significant learning. We believe that both components of the curriculum have to be unified in a dynamic whole, where theoretical and practical knowledge are in a continuous reciprocity, with each sphere of knowledge informing the other.

A general framework of theoretical knowledge is a necessary and useful component of curricula, for it can create cognitive and metacognitive conflicts in students' minds. Moreover, when it is interrelated to practice, theory is connected with meaning and context. It is therefore useful to verify students' beliefs, to support and clarify the act of teaching, to broaden the students' conceptions, and to contextualize the experience of the teaching act.

However, we contend that the starting and end points in teacher training should be in the teaching act itself. Indeed, from a constructivist point of view, learning means searching for meaning and making sense in terms of what has already been experienced and is already known. Learning is an active and subjective process in which students construct knowledge and draw on their personal background experiences to make sense. In short, the principle of integration presupposes the development of autonomous, critical and responsible thinking.

Studies on Lipman and Sharp's pedagogy, have shown that a philosophical community of inquiry can foster children's higher-order thinking skills. Concerning preservice teachers, we postulate that learning how to think philosophically about pedagogical and epistemological realities could help preservice teachers integrate the diversity of theories they are receiving at university and to combine them with their own teaching practice.

Community of Inquiry

Philosophy is not understood here in its traditional meaning. Its essence is not found in dogmatism nor in 'truths' gathered into deep and immutable formula. On the contrary, the role of philosophy is to question, to doubt, to criticize, to clarify, to explain ideas and beliefs that are at the basis of human activities. In this sense, doing philosophy means developing a natural curiosity and sense of wonder, becoming aware of the ambiguities, contradictions and problems that exist in society, and developing the motivation to act positively on it.

Sheedy writes that philosophy is not an activity reserved for a few professional philosophers, but concerns any practitioner. Indeed, by constructing a personal conception of her or his professional field of action and by developing a personal interpretation of this universe, the practitioner is 'doing' philosophy, for she or he questions in a critical manner some fundamental elements of her or his field. Actually, we understand philosophy as a 'critical and responsible reflexion with peers' about professional practice and educational theories. Critical reflexion helps prospective teachers 'to distance themselves from their own practice and so create enough analytic space for reflection on this practice'. However, critical reflexion by itself is incomplete. Caring thinking can help teachers to choose appropriate solutions when confronted with social and moral dilemmas within their daily practice. Studies show that the community of inquiry can contribute to the development of caring thinking.

Working with philosophical concepts fosters higher-order thinking skills. Indeed, to understand them and to construct the logic of their structure as well as their meanings, the participants have to reason, translate and get involved in research. Also, philosophical concepts such as the self, the body, the mind, culture, education, relationships, and so on, are universal. In this sense, they are consistent with the person's fundamental interests and personal experiences and, for this reason, motivate students to 'struggle' with them. The knowledge that is then acquired by the prospective teachers does not come from outside, but from inside the self and, consequently, is significant.

Finally, the introduction of philosophical concepts into teacher training programs is quite educative, for once a person gets interested in the search for an ever better meaning, she or he is on a royal road to develop personal, social and political consciousness. In short, the philosophical community of inquiry is a social vehicle which may lead to the development of autonomous, critical and responsible thinking, for it works at three levels: first, it is a method of personal and collective investigation of problems, involving students in the posing and solving of problems; second, it is an educational process, for it helps students to become aware of these problems and to analyze critically their causes and consequences through structured dialogues and interactions; third, it leads to action.

Methodology

The methodology that we advocate consists of five steps:

1) being conscious of problematic and ambiguous situations in teaching physical education and keeping note of it in a reflexive journal;
2) sharing the written reflexions with the members of the community of inquiry;
3) raising philosophical questions about the pedagogical problems that have been presented to us;
4) engaging in a philosophical dialogue about it within the community of inquiry;
5) acting positively on pedagogical reality.

Step 1: Preservice teachers are suggested to keep a reflexive journal (log) in which they write their own reflections and questions, and in which they describe, in detail, significant events that happened during their lesson. For the preservice teachers, this represents an opportunity to become aware of their thinking and to develop the habit of metareflection on their ways of doing and being while teaching physical education. Being conscious of a problem, question or particular situation is the first step in solving, answering, or improving it.

Step 2: The reflexive logs serve as the novels in Lipman and Sharp's approach. Instead of engaging the philosophicopedagogical dialogue with the reading of a novel, each preservice teacher is invited to read aloud a part of her or his reflexion. Other participants are listening; they can take notes. The preservice teachers are, in turn, actor, writer, story-teller, and listener and cooperator.

Step 3: Once everyone has presented their reflexion about an epistemological concept or pedagogical situation, the community of inquiry proceeds with the gathering of philosophical comments or questions that the previous steps may have raised in the participants' minds. Are there two or three persons who felt the same feeling, to whom the same problem happened, who wonder about the same theory, and so on? If so, the participants may decide to organize a dialogue on it; or they may organize it around any ambiguity or conflictual situation that has been presented to the group.

Step 4: The next step is the philosophical dialogue about the topic that has been chosen by the preservice teachers. A philosophico-pedagogical dialogue is characterized by the following elements:

— the concepts that are discussed by the group have their origin in a personal and concrete problematic situation;
— the problematic situation is shared with the group not only in a descriptive fashion, but in a reflexive one. This means that it causes the participants to question, wonder, doubt or, in other words, to have cognitive conflicts;
— the dialogue is mainly involved with why the problem exists. By reflecting on the whys of the problem, the community investigates the concrete and complex social and pedagogical reality of physical education in which they live and teach, but which they may not thoroughly understand;
— because the participants meet in a large community of inquiry, the dialogue is characterized by pluralism.

This implies that the exposed doubt or conflict is answered by a variety of solutions, interpretations and perspectives - which all come from a personal construction and conception of epistemology and pedagogy. It requires autonomous thinking;

— although any comment might be useful to the enrichment of the community of inquiry, all comments might not be accepted. Philosophical dialogue should never be characterized by laxism or relativism, but rather by the individual's efforts to reach a pertinent and meaningful construction. In this sense, it should be grounded on good reasons or built on sound justifications;

— even then, not all grounded justifications can be accepted to solve a problem.

The variety of contexts play an important role in pedagogy. Moreover, pedagogical problems usually involve children that is, unique people. In this sense, the justifications have to be critical that is, sensitive to the context. Preservice teachers often lack the skills and knowledge for a critical analysis of their pedagogical situation. This is why this step becomes so fundamental. The community of inquiry is the locus where they can gradually learn to solve their pedagogical problems. Indeed, preservice teachers are invited to reflect on the why of their problems and construct their own solutions. In doing so, the participants are prompted to look for the theories that they have learned, examine them in a critical manner, and build on this to develop their own theories and solutions to problems. Discussing pedagogical and epistemological questions in a philosophical manner is not an easy task. It is the professor's role to guide preservice teachers.

Step 5. The philosophical community of inquiry should enable preservice teachers to create their own relationships between theories and pedagogical problems, in order to improve their teaching actions. However, the improvement of action is a never-ending process. This means that what has resulted from the dialogue within the philosophico-pedagogical community of inquiry should be considered as a mere hypothesis of solutions that may fit or may not fit in with the reality of the class. The solutions found within the community of inquiry should not be applied as 'band-aids' to the problems, but should serve as a starting point for further reflection about why and how one can contribute to the improvement of the pedagogical experience in physical education. Having identified and investigated important situations in their personal and pedagogical experience, preservice teachers should be more able to decide how to use the knowledge and skills gained.

By treating preservice teachers as objects to be counted, as machines to be developed and controlled, traditional teacher training programs reflect marginalizing social conditions which cause prospective teachers to relinquish their capacity to make real choices and to be cut out of meaningful decision-making. The collective processes of reflection in the community help rebuild the capacity of teachers and prospective teachers to be creative actors in the world.

5

Storytelling in PE Teacher Training

Much of human life is conducted through story. We make sense of our experiences by telling the stories that we live, and we learn about other lives by hearing the stories that others tell. Stories capture the richness and nuances of meaning in everyday existence and give insight into the complexity of our experiences. Narrative is about the telling of stories.

In taking a postmodern perspective it is understood that ways of understanding ourselves in relation to physical activity constitute our sense of self. It is produced through a range of meaning-making and social practices which vary and sometimes contradict. As individuals negotiate and position themselves around physical activity they develop a sense of self that is shaped and embodied by the stories of their physical experiences. It is also understood that these positions are fluid and plural rather than static and resistant to change. People then have a degree of personal agency over who they are and how they understand their physical self.

Those drawn to the profession of PE have generally developed a positive and unproblematic relationship with physical activity, sport and the meanings made around PE. For many, sport has played a central role in their lives and a significant basis for identity construction. Hence, traditional ways of thinking and speaking about concepts such as individualism, meritocracy and technocratic rationality are seen by many as 'fair and equitable', as is sport itself. In order to develop critical perspectives in relation to teaching and learning in PE it is important to understand how 'other' individuals construct and make meaning in relation to physical activity.

Critical Pedagogies

In traditional educational theory, the existing arrange-ment of society is taken as given and schools are seen as rationally distributing education in what is perceived as a basically just society. In contrast, critical educational theory recognizes that social and institutional practices operate within a society that is characterized by relations of power and domination, a society where individuals do not have equal opportunities to learn or live.

A critical pedagogy is one that resists the reprodu-ction of the status quo by uncovering relations of domination and opening up spaces for voices that are usually suppressed in and through traditional practices. Weiler argues that the critical educator thus 'takes as central the inner histories and experiences of the students themselves' and seeks to foster a critical reflection of their everyday experiences.

While critical pedagogy is not readily summed up in a phrase, generally it seeks to move beyond interpretation of cultural constructs to a point of 'change' or 'action'. A critical pedagogy questions taken-for-granted assum-ptions and practices that support the dominant culture and ignore the lived experiences of those marginalized or different. While researchers continue to highlight the systematic and inequitable effects of schooling whereby particular groups are advantaged and others simultaneously disadvantaged, schools and therefore teachers still have the potential to either perpetuate or confront these effects.

Teachers in particular can be powerful in shaping student perceptions of wider society, their place and their sense of self through the curriculum, pedagogical choices and the nature of the relationships they foster with students in their care. Such a perspective recognizes the agency of teachers and advocates a teacher education curriculum that 'links the critical study of power, language, culture and history to the practice of a critical pedagogy, one that values student experience and student voice'.

For Giroux and McLaren, voice is a key element in critical pedagogy. By valuing student voice, focus can be directed to the meanings students make of their schooling experiences. Voice also alerts us to the way that all meaning-making is situated historically and mediated culturally. Student voice can be shared through stories.

Critical pedagogies are not teaching methods. Rather, teachers are asked to confront their beliefs and to question taken-for-granted assumptions around difference. They are encouraged to adopt critical frames of reference in order to interrogate their teaching and identify the knowledge and skills being valued, the groups being privileged and what is happening for those who are different. Within PE, critical pedagogies seek to move practice beyond the reproduction of elitist, gendered and exclusive ideologies toward more inclusive and socially just practice.

The kind of discourse children experience in physical education deeply affects their thought processes and, hence, the nature of what is learned. This relates not only to learning defined narrowly in terms of particular skills or techniques but also to students' whole sense of the possibilities and meanings of the subject.

However, in the context of dominant practices that work to powerfully reproduce PE as essentially a domain of elitist, exclusionist and technocratic tradition, putting critical pedagogy into action can be confronting and challenging in the least. Whilst issues related to social justice have become part of the professional dialogue and curriculum documents in PE, Tinning suggests that there are still considerable tensions in delivering a socially critical curriculum in the context of schools that increasingly align themselves with the ethics of the corporate world.

In attempting to offer a 'collective emancipation' from the oppressions of gender, race, class and ability binaries, critical pedagogies can be set up for failure in the practical setting. Against this background of critique, theorists have called for less utopian pedagogies that do not make promises of 'emancipation for all' but rather move toward practices that connect with an individual's freedom and opportunity to participate in a movement culture. In this sense a critical pedagogy would orient ways of thinking about a socially just education and seek to develop an emotional commitment to 'doing things differently'. One tool for the development of this commitment is critical storytelling.

Storytelling

Telling stories has been an accepted mode of constructing reality throughout human history. Story is a natural and common mode of thinking. We live storied lives and build stories through our life experiences. Stories have long been used as both a means to express cultural identity and a vehicle for communication. However, more recently narrative and stories are appearing as legitimate forms of inquiry and knowledge construction. In narrative inquiry, stories are used to describe human experience and connect us with others. In clarification, Connelly and Clandinin remind us that, while the phenomenon is 'story', the form of inquiry is 'narrative'. This implies that 'people by nature lead storied lives and tell stories of those lives, whereas narrative researchers describe such lives, collect and tell stories of them, and write narratives of experience'. Through stories, researchers gain powerful insights into the complex subjective reality of the individual and the manner in which they interpret and create meaning in their lives. In health care, stories have been used as a strategy to develop skills in clinical settings and assist nurses to understand the lived experiences of their patients.

Storytelling has also been used as a strategy for social change where feminists and other groups rely on the oppressed telling the stories of their daily lives. In the field of sport and PE, the use of narrative in the form of stories is emerging as a strong methodological tool that offers a deeper appreciation of life within these cultural contexts. Significant researchers include Sparkes, Denison, Lyons and Oliver, whose work with PE teachers, athletes and children provides evidence of the potential of these methods to enhance understanding of the diverse ways in which self-understandings and physicality develop for these groups.

Ccritical strategy

In an educational context the critical aspect of stories is expressed through giving voice to students. The appeal of stories lies in their ability to capture interest and bring ideas to life in personal scenarios. Perspectives that focus on voice, testimony, autobiography and memory are vital because they carve out spaces for the embodied voice of the silenced. Stories graphically illustrate how privilege and difference affect the lives of real people. Storytelling can also be a negotiation of power. By giving voice to previously silenced groups, and by describing the diversity of their experiences, readers gain insight into their own practices, experience and bias. If human subjectivities are fragmented then it follows that stories do not necessarily represent some sort of essential truth or understanding. However, by drawing on memories, either partial or fragmented as an attempt to uncover 'strands of experiences and to understand them in new and different ways', stories have much to offer in terms of developing more socially just or critical pedagogies.

As we come to better understand students' and teachers' stories, their interpretations of experiences, we may be able to better understand what we need to or ought to do, and as teacher educators and researchers that is our moral obligation. Critical stories provide a means and opportunity to make sense of cultural practices in alternative ways. When we hear stories, we are given opportunities to critically interrogate our own histories and values. We can create parallels and connections with other peoples' stories or contrast and contradiction, both of which lead to a deeper understanding of the multiple ways that meaning is constructed around any particular cultural practice.

In the context of social change, Razack suggests that the process of storytelling works to share alternatives to knowledge and experiences of the world that are not admitted into dominant paradigms. The critical element in storytelling focuses on the voices that are silenced through traditional education in order to interrogate the actions, processes and complex ways in which relations of domination are sustained, lived and resisted. Ellsworth suggests that as practising teachers we should work hard at critically examining what we share with those who share their stories with us. We must work from the basis that we only have partial knowledge and come from different storied lives.

For teachers of PE, this kind of critical gaze can generate insights into the ways in which the social construction of sport and physical activity has material consequences for those positioned as 'not sporty'. In the present study narrative inquiry was used to explore issues around engagement in a physical culture for girls. The resulting stories provide a powerful medium that graphically illustrate how concepts such as competence, gender and difference affect the lives of real people.

Storytelling for PETE Students

Those attracted to the profession of PE have generally had an unproblematic relationship with PE, sport and physical activity. Increasingly, they come from similar economic, cultural and sporting backgrounds and are often products of PE programmes where all physical activities were assumed under the umbrella of sport. Generally they have excelled in these areas and accept many of the traditional practices including the central place of sport within the curriculum. Their understanding of the institution of sport is overwhelmingly positive and uncritical. While some shift and make sense of teacher training to a point where they can critically interrogate their practices, generally their personal identities provide filters that mediate the adoption of new or alternative approaches. In deflecting rather than engaging with critical perspectives, many attribute 'students who are not into PE' to youth becoming lazy rather than the possibility that sport might be based on elitist, masculine and competitive premises.

Brown believes that many go to the classroom or field with sedimented practices similar to those of their professional mentors. Kirk and Tinning suggest that, within their ideology, teaching is often a technical process where subject matter and strategies are based on intended objectives. It is not surprising then that researchers have found student teachers of PE to be less concerned with issues of social justice and equality than the technical skills of teaching, which are often seen as ends in themselves. Few have gender sensitivities and often identify girls as the 'problem' in PE. Even fewer can be convinced of alternatives to sport that are not based on traditional notions of strength, speed and competition.

Given their background and identity positions, it can be difficult for training PE teachers to embrace the notion or see the need for a critical pedagogy. Tinning in particular suggests that, in drawing on personal histories to make sense of their teaching practice, many training teachers find the intellectual rationale for a change insufficient to alter either their perception or practice. Further to this, the process of adapting to the uncertainty and complexity of critical approaches demands a kind of unlearning and risk-taking which can be confronting in the least.

In maintaining technical and concrete approaches to teaching, they position themselves within a modernist paradigm where outcomes can be measurable and 'real'. So too, in the absence of alternative courses of action or assistance in making sense of the complexity of teaching, they are limited in their capacity to engage with critical perspectives. However, it is still important to put student teachers into situations that challenge their beliefs and knowledge so they can begin to resolve the contradictions they experience within the frame and support of teacher education programmes.

In the context of PE teacher preparation programmes, the process of storytelling can create a safe context for student teachers to focus on lived experiences and challenge taken-for-granted understandings. It can provide an opportunity to live though another's experience and reveal worlds that are otherwise closed. Armour and Fernandez-Balboa argue for a connective understanding of pedagogy that 'consolidate our identities jointly with those who share the classroom with us'. When connections are made to real and lived experiences, learners can build meaningful connections, which are important for deep understanding and authentic learning.

The research

This research is concerned with the influence of young women's experiences as lived, interpreted and expressed through story on PE student teachers' appreciation of diversity and orientation towards critical pedagogies. In the context of the final year of both a primary and secondary teaching degree 'stories of physicality' were presented to student teachers with the intention of encouraging an appreciation for the multiple subjectivities developed in relation to physical activity for young women.

Participants for the study consisted of a cohort of final year student teachers who would go on to teach health and PE in the secondary education sector in South Australia and a group of final year primary general teachers who would complete a generalist primary degree with a specialization in health and physical education (HPE).

During the preceding years both cohorts had already been exposed to courses that addressed student diversity and critical approaches. Within their final HPE course student teachers from both cohorts were required to plan explicitly for equity issues within their teaching. Numbers included 28 female and 32 male student teachers ranging in age from 20 to 28 years. Two female teacher educators who presented the courses in which the stories were embedded were also interviewed as part of the research process. Though this was their first experience using stories, both were teacher educators with more than 10 years' experience and were committed to the development of critical approaches to teaching and learning.

The construction of the stories occurred in a previous study that investigated the personal experiences of a group of young women regarding their body, gender and physical activity. Through the mutual construction of a story, attempt was made to create a cameo of a personal yet significant experience or series of experiences in the life of the young woman, specifically related to physical activity. Coauthoring is a method that feminists have employed in order to relinquish some of the control researchers have over the research agenda and knowledge produced from it.

The stories in this research were coauthored in that the form and content of each story emerged from a collaborative effort between the young woman and researcher, the purpose of which was to share meaning and understand phenomena. The model of storytelling involved collapsing detailed conversation around a specific issue or series of events into a 'cameo' or personal story. This was done with the intention of capturing the style and basic nature of the participant's discussion. Stories were crafted with the young women concerned to form a representation that closely mirrored their own voice.

The resulting 'stories of physicality' highlight the complex processes that occur as young women negotiate physical activity. They identify discursive, social and institutional practices, which enhance or inhibit the development of a physical identity for some young people. Five stories were selected for use in this study and were chosen on the basis that they represented a range of personal experiences and subjectivities around physical activity. While complete versions of the stories can be found in previous works, the following statements present a brief overview of each story, although they convey little of the complexity of the individuals' physical identities as communicated in the complete stories.

Diana. Diana's story was created around a young woman whose physical identity was closely tied to achievement in karate. Even though it was a non-traditional activity for girls, Diana found the subculture of karate more supportive of her physical endeavours than she had previously experienced at school. Diana hated PE, hated the way the boys teased her and hated running, though she now prefers to train with the guys because they 'work harder'. Diana stated in her story 'I'm the highest belt in my class which gives me a sense of power and people look up to me.'

Kerry. Kerry's story conveys a damaged physical identity resulting from an embodied sense of not measuring up the cultural ideal of a thin body. Kerry felt that her whole life would be better if her body was different. She felt ignored in PE settings but at the same time she worked hard at 'not being noticed'. Kerry didn't enjoy PE, especially in the way that she was left till last when teams were picked and the way that she felt her body was always on display. She commented in her story that 'I'd definitely be happier if I were smaller. My whole life would be different.'

Maree. Maree's story presents an image of a young woman who actively resisted traditionally gendered behaviours and sporting activities. In playing football, she positioned herself outside traditional gendered expectations but still as a team person. She felt that those around her disregarded her achievements and questioned her 'need to succeed'. Maree enjoyed PE because it provided an opportunity to be physical and strong but was reminded that 'Football is only for the boys. They don't say it to your face but you can tell.'

Amanda. Amanda's story talks of a young woman for whom PE had been a source of humiliation and alienation where she felt painfully aware that she was not skilled, strong or fit. She worked to passively resist active opportunities, thus compounding her sense of inadequacy and lack of physical skills. Amanda learnt to be invisible in PE and activity contexts. She felt that 'You were just supposed to know everything before you set foot on the oval.'

Lori. Lori's story presents the voice of a 'comfortable' body, one that was contented with herself, her gender and her physical ability. Lori's physical experiences had been well supported and she was provided with plenty of opportunities to develop motor skills and physical abilities. Lori thrived on basketball as it kept her fit and 'toned'. For Lori, female athletes should be able to play well but should also look 'feminine'. Lori comments in her story that 'There is so much pressure on girls to be thin. Guys do it. If you are not slim then you are not attractive.'

Procedures

The stories were presented to student teachers within two courses that were linked to a series of 'lab school' or micro teaching episodes. In both the primary and secondary training programmes, the courses were primarily aimed at developing skills of critical reflection, which were tackled in a number of ways both practically and theoretically. An underpinning principle of both courses was the notion that 'teaching is about dealing with complexity' and both teacher educators believed that student teachers should be immersed in this complexity.

The teacher educators were asked to integrate the stories into their final year courses and monitor the influences of their use with student teachers. The stories were incorporated into courses with the intention to problematize traditional practices around PE and to generate views on the ways in which values to physical activity can be established and maintained. They were available to students through the university's online course delivery system. Student teachers were asked to analyse the content of the stories and focus on the central themes. They were then asked to respond to the stories in terms of identifying the positions and feelings of the storyteller as well as considering the implications of the stories on their own teaching and learning practices.

Student teachers were invited to move beyond a point of interpretation of the stories to identify (actions they could take) pedagogies, which might create real change, challenge or support for the storyteller. They were instructed to write their responses to these tasks onto the web page that was shared with a student group of three and the teacher educators involved. The purpose of the discussion group was to share individuals' ideas as well as hear how others had interpreted the stories. Each student teacher was asked to respond to three of the five stories over the course of ten weeks. In the final week student teachers were also asked to reflect on the storytelling process as a whole, particularly the influence of the stories on their thinking and planning for teaching. Whilst student teachers were informed that their reflections would be used in a research project they were not specifically graded.

Data Collection and Analysis

Data for this study included student teacher online written responses to the story tasks which were downloaded from the group web pages as word documents, as well as teacher educator interview data. Interviews were based on a qualitative theoretical framework. The fundamental principle of qualitative interviewing is to provide a framework within which respondents can express their own understandings in their own terms'. Interviews were semistructured and conversational in nature. Lead questions were designed to elicit responses from the two teacher educators around the storytelling process, the timing, the meanings students made of the stories and the influence of the stories on both student responses and lab school practice. Interviews were conducted by the researcher for one hour on two occasions. They were audio-taped and transcribed verbatim for qualitative analysis. Both teacher educators listened to each of the interview tapes and scrutinized the transcriptions in order to verify their accuracy.

Information gathered from interviews and student responses were compiled to form a composite of participant views regarding the storytelling process. The purpose of the data analysis was to reflect on the participants' perspectives and interpret findings through the creation of categories and themes. Analytic induction is the process of drawing themes and commonalities from data and is a suitable way to ascertain the experiences and thoughts of participants. In this study the data collected from both sources were inductively analysed and coded to identify statements that related to the way student teachers made connections with the stories as well as the ways in which the stories had influenced student teacher thinking and action around teaching and learning.

By drawing on the data, outcomes of the storytelling process for training teachers became apparent. The findings of this study are presented around the descriptive themes that evolved from the storytelling process, including the power and influence of the stories as well as the meanings and messages that evolved from them for student teachers. Deeper analysis focused on student teacher engagement with critical perspectives and ranged from describing and informing storytellers' experiences to shifts toward taking responsibility for difference and reconstructing practice in ways that might better accommodate diverse learners. A member check with the two teacher educators involved allowed them to react to the researcher's first analysis of categories and themes by suggesting alternative interpretations to further enhance the trustworthiness of the researcher's analysis. They suggested no changes during the member check.

Working with Stories

When describing the influence of the stories on their thinking, student teachers responded in various ways. While some felt the power of the stories was connected to its 'realness', others were able to read the story 'as if they were part of it', which encouraged deeper connections, different perspectives and the development of empathy towards the storyteller.

Realness

The stories proved cathartic for those individuals who vividly recalled similar personal experiences around physical activity. In these situations, a strong emotional connection was formed between the data and their comments on the implications of the stories for teaching and learning. Importantly though, for many student teachers the significance of the stories came from the fact that they were being told by 'real people' or potential students in their classes.

Because the story is from someone who is real. They could reflect the stories of the children in your class. In a number of cases, the stories seemed to generate discussion about how the person within the story would feel. If student teachers could relate and access these emotional links to the storyteller then the story seemed to have greater impact on thinking around teaching and learning. Because it's a message from someone. A story from a real person has quite a lot of power in terms of being able to 'see' the story as if you were the person within it. They seemed to generate a lot of emotions about how that person would feel and that makes it have a stronger impact. Particularly if they (student teachers) are reading a story that contains either something they have experienced or a friend or they can relate, there is an emotional link and the connection to seeing the need for doing things differently is stronger.

Different Perspectives

Both teacher educators saw the stories as a way of encouraging student teachers to see the teaching process from a different perspective and to understand a broader range of outcomes stemming from experiences in PE. They were keen for student teachers to focus on student learning as much as teacher action and realize that some teaching practices can be potentially harmful despite good intentions. In so doing, they believed the stories encouraged student teachers to consider the ways in which dominant practices around PE could exclude, marginalize and alienate rather than include all children. Alice (teacher educator) commented that 'the stories were a way of getting them (student teachers) to see things from a different perspective' and Viv (teacher educator) felt that 'the stories really develop empathy for the diversity in learners that they are going to work with'.

Developing Empathy

Empathy is about an attempt to understand, to experience, to feel things as another human person understands, experiences and feels. It involves imaginatively inhabiting the world of another person, rather than imaging one's own experiences. Both teacher educators felt that the stories contributed towards the development of empathy in their student teachers in that they encouraged a vision of PE from the perspective of the storyteller.

The stories also gave student teachers permission to talk about their own experiences, both positive and negative, around sport and PE. In this way, individuals developed further resonances with what the storyteller had to say. If student teachers could make emotional connections with the storyteller then their embodied reactions were more likely to enhance their empathy with the storyteller and recall of their own experiences.

Meanings and Messages

The stories provided a catalyst to explore a number of issues around teaching and learning in PE. In their group talk and web page submissions, student teachers identi-fied a number of messages that emerged from the stories, including the importance of seeing and noticing what was happening for girls in their classes, as well as the notion that PE can be a form of public display. For a number of student teachers the stories also affirmed the need for particular pedagogies to ensure that all students feel safe in their classes.

Noticing Girls

Student teachers believed the stories allowed them to develop increasing awareness around outcomes for girls in their classes. While their web comments indicated a growing appreciation of diversity, some individuals went further than descriptions of the differences that they were noticing in their classes to finding reasons for these differences. For example, girls were described not only in terms of what 'they could and could not do', but also in terms 'how they came to be'. In this way student teachers were beginning to demonstrate an 'informing' level of critical reflection where they attempted to understand the nature of the differences in ability and outcome witnessed in their classes. Sara (student teacher) believed 'the stories allowed us to think more deeply and understand perspectives around gender in particular' and Sue (student teacher) commented that 'the girls don't really come with the same set of skills but it's not their fault'.

As the stories were all constructed around the experiences of adolescent females, they served to shed light on a number of issues for girls in the PE learning environment. Understandings around gender emerged for student teachers in various ways.

While some acknowledged that the language they used with students was 'probably not gender inclusive' others commented more broadly that they had not previously considered how girls might 'feel' in their classes. Whilst it was easy to identify girls as a 'problem' in PE due to their lack of success and engagement, Sam (student teacher) commented that 'It's interesting to see how girls think' and Ivan (student teacher) suggested that 'It seems that some girls learn not to like PE'. Consideration of the gendered experiences communicated in the stories stimulated discussion around the nature of activities within a PE curriculum. A number of student teachers indicated in their responses that PE activities should be connected in some way with the students' interests, backgrounds and abilities. Carol's story (karate) in particular initiated consideration of the need to make links with what students do outside of school hours in order to celebrate those skills and abilities within the school context.

Public Display

Student teachers also acknowledged that all physical activity is a form of public display. This developed awareness of how PE practices could place learners 'on show' and was quite different from classroom practice where work is private and errors are not necessarily visible. Their responses highlighted the need for strategies that reduced a learner's sense of being 'watched' or critically gazed upon. The theme of not putting students 'on show' came through strongly in their commentary - as did the awareness of self-esteem damage that could occur through poorly constructed and managed learning experiences. As Will suggested, 'It's important that we don't put kids on show when they are learning things. It can be disastrous.' Whilst the stories involved in this study were the stories of adolescent girls, student teachers in both cohorts suggested that issues raised in the stories were not necessarily concerns for girls alone. In particular, it was identified that issues centred on competition, public display and comparison with others were problematic for both males and females. Student teachers identified that competition in PE meant different things for different students. Whilst some students might be spurred on by the physical contest, others as indicated in the stories could be alienated by constant comparisons with peers.

Particular Pedagogies

According to responses, the stories also signified and or reinforced the need for particular pedagogies and approaches to teaching and learning that were promoted in other ways through the teaching programme. In particular, student teachers reiterated the need for ensuring success for children in their care but were careful to point out, like Sean, that success 'might mean different things for different learners'. Emma felt success was made possible by including students in decisions made around curriculum choices 'to make sure all students have input and are recognised', while Kate suggested it was important to 'know students and find out about them'. Michael commented that it was important to 'make winning different for different kids'.

In attempting to provide for success Kayla and Michael both identified the need for appropriate activities in order to develop skills and increase a sense of confidence that learners have over their own physical capacities. However, Sean commented that what a teacher thought appropriate and what students think appropriate 'might be two different things', and used Amanda's story to point out that 'being forced to do an activity' could have dire consequences for some learners. In Diana's story, student teachers identified the problematic nature of 'just throwing kids into games'. It was deemed that large-sided games in particular could set some students up for failure by not providing adequate opportunity to learn the skills required to be successful in game settings. So too in attempting to mediate the public performance of PE that was identified in Kerry and Amanda's stories, student teachers suggested that small-sided activities might work to increase participation while not placing learners in a position where they feel they are on show. This was reiterated by one of the teacher educators.

> The stories reinforced what we have talked about in terms of having small-sided activities and practices and ensuring that success is paramount. Being sensitive to the fact that in physical activity and physical education people are on show, it's different from the classroom where the 'work' is more private and errors in particular are more private.

Generally the stories encouraged broader notions and understandings around safety in PE as evidenced by responses that drew attention to emotional and social safety in the same way as physical safety might be considered. Similarly, responses identified practices that compromised the safety of particular children. They made connections between teacher action or inaction and the safety of the children in their care. Implicit in their dialogue was an attempt by the student teachers to take responsibility for the learning environment created in PE.

Engagement with Critical Pedagogies

Growth for student teachers in terms of engagement with critical pedagogies became evident at different levels. For some, a critical orientation was evidenced in an appreciation for the broader learning outcomes that could be attributed to PE.

Others were moving towards taking greater responsibility for equity and having things happen in their lessons that explicitly catered for and valued difference. This was especially evident in comments that identified specific change or action that could be taken and represented a jump from the conceptual to the real. Whilst a number of student teachers identified that they did not necessarily have the answers to complex issues around gender equity, they could identify that change needed to be real and 'more than just talk'. This seemed more apparent for those who focused specifically on issues of gender in their lab school where they could generate real strategies that catered for difference and embed them into their practice. Sian's group planned activities that required some level of cooperation as well as physical prowess and actively encouraged and 'expected' the girls to do their best in all of the activities.

Both teacher educators believed that the stories supported this growth in that they enabled contemplation of issues without feeling the pressure of finding immediate solutions.If student teachers are introduced to these concepts along the way then they do become more embedded in their way of thinking and while they don't necessarily have all of the answers they know what questions to ask.

Growth in terms of a critical perspective was also evident in student teachers' commitment toward actively dealing with discrimination or harassment. Rather than accepting various student behaviours as a sign of diversity, a number of student responses indicated that they would actively deal with any sort of behaviour that might directly or indirectly alienate other students from learning in the best way possible.

While the stories permitted student teachers to explore issues, their own histories, values and positions, engagement with critical pedagogies still depended on how student teachers heard these stories and the ways in which their own subject positions came together to create moments of insight. Whereas some were able to interrogate their own histories as well as the institution of PE itself, others only managed this in superficial ways. Viv (teacher educator) commented that 'some are still very uncritical of the institutions of physical education and sport'. Moreover, Kim (student teacher) did not see the point of the stories.

Storytelling does not guarantee that student teachers will connect with or understand the nature of diversity within their student groups. Stories are not always empowering. Without the mechanisms to critique stories, individuals were not able to identify strategies and determine effective action or reconstruct PE in different ways. So, too, the strategies of dialogue and voice do not work as neatly as they might because the various histories of student teachers are not left behind when they attempt to critically reflect. Kayla (student teacher) felt the process quite confronting in that 'there are too many things for beginning teachers to deal with and this means more'. However, critically reflecting on one's own positions with similarities or differences to the stories told still allows insights into the ways in which the social construct of 'ability' has real material consequences for those who are positioned as less able.

6

Changing Trends in PE Teacher Training

One of the things that receives much attention in the realistic approach to teacher education, is that we cannot understand teacher change if considered merely from a cognitive stance. Teaching is a profession in which feelings and emotions play an essential role. The problem of educational change, and particularly of teacher education, is first of all a problem of dealing with the natural emotional reactions of human beings to the threat of losing certainty, predictability or stability.

This affective dimension is too much neglected in the technical-rationality approach. For example, most literature on the role of preconceptions guiding student teachers' actions tend to focus on just one type of human information processing. This type of information processing—mostly focused on by teacher educators—can be described as rational or logical. For example, student teachers are asked to analyse the goals of a lesson they gave, the way they worked towards these goals and the effects. The impact of such approaches on the student teachers' preconceptions is relatively low, as the situations these student teachers are confronted with during their teaching practice, elicit a lot of feelings (for example feelings of fear), concerns, value conflicts, etcetera, which are certainly not only rational, logical, cognitive or conscious and easily remain outside the analysis.

People do not act solely on the basis of logical and rational analysis. Feelings of fear can be very influential, "washing out" any rational intentions formulated before the lesson. Very often one sees such a student teacher fall back on very old patterns, partly influenced by survival behaviour developed during the student teacher's own personal history, and partly influenced by stored images of other teachers handling severe classroom problems.

Realistic Approach to Teacher Training

The realistic approach to teacher education not only has consequences for the types of interventions teacher educators should use to promote the intended learning process in the student teachers, but there are also consequences on the organisational level of teacher education curricula. First of all linking theory and practice requires frequent alternation of school teaching days and meetings at the teacher education institute. Secondly, in order to harmonise the interventions of school-based mentors and institute-based teacher educators, close cooperation between the schools and the institute is necessary. Not every school may be suitable as a practicum site: the school must be able to offer a sound balance between safety and challenge and a balance between the goal of serving student teachers' learning and the interests of the school.Thirdly, the approach advocated here implies that it is impossible to make a clear distinction between different subjects in the teacher education programme. The realistic approach "is not compatible with a programme structure showing separate modules such as 'subject matter methods', 'general education', 'psychology of learning', etc. Teacher knowledge which is assumed to function in practice is knowledge based on experiences; and teaching experiences are not as fragmented as the programmes of many teacher education institutes would suggest."Finally, the realistic approach in teacher education requires specific competencies from both teacher educators and cooperating teachers. This implies the need for professional development of teacher education staff and cooperating teachers in the school.

The realistic approach is based on the following tenets:

— It starts from concrete practical problems and the concerns experienced by (student) teachers in real contexts.

— It aims at the promotion of systematic reflection of (student) teachers on their own and their students' wanting, feeling, thinking and acting, on the role of context, and on the relationships between those aspects.

— It builds on the personal interaction between the teacher educator and the (student) teacher and on the interaction amongst the (student) teachers.

— It takes gestalts of teacher as the starting point for professional learning, which has consequences for the kind of theory that is offered (Theory with capital T versus theory with a small t).

— It has a strongly integrated character. Two types of integration are involved: integration of theory and practice and integration of several disciplines.

Technical teachers' training is going on in both full-time and part-time or correspondence courses in technical higher education. The students are adults and in the correspondence courses, they are very often already over thirty. Thus, age is one of the main general features of this training. The other feature is that they are already graduates. There are some specific aspects:

1. Methods and attitudes considered useful for a teacher, not only for an engineer,
2. They are students, very often teachers and parents at the same time,
3. They fulfil many kinds of roles at the same time, often similar to each other, often in different aspects of life,
4. They have a stable personality.

We know from educational psychology that training adults is more effective if the adult students can:

1. reveal their needs to be taught,
2. participate in discussing and solving problems,
3. decide the goal,
4. take part in defining requirements during learning,
5. realise their former experiences,
6. understand that learning and studying are intrinsic processes,
7. be open to every opinion,
8. be responsible for their learning,
9. be willing to change their mind, way of thinking,
10. affect the teaching method, the teaching process, and the time-table employed.

Moreover, it is important in training adults—both in graduate and undergraduate training—that we should aspire to co-operative partnership based on open communication, instead of subordinated traditional student-teacher relationship. It is very important to make clear that the achievement of the students is more important than that of the teachers.

Successful learning is possible only if the experiences and the knowledge are synthetised with the new information received in the courses. It means that in the teaching-learning process the student group, community is primary, it is them who play the main role, instead of the teacher. Students' activity is one of the most significant requirements toward the training. Spontaneous activity is created in group or teamwork in co-operation with others in a constant exchange of information and the common shaping of opinions. To develop the ability of group co-operation in group work—starting with the experiences of the adults participating in training—it is important to analyse and discuss professional problems together, to set up alternatives, and to give reasons for the decisions reached. In this case the teacher has to help or assist only, and should not give solutions. The education should be basically student-centered. We have to make the adult student responsible for his own development in the teaching process.

Curriculum Development

Unless we are specialists in curriculum-development of physical education teacher training, we know, that a psychologically and professionally well planned curriculum, and methodology can meet the requirements of training. Some of them are as follows:

— if possible, applicants must perform an aptitude test or take part in an interview aiming
— to raise the knowledge (basic level) of the students to a sufficient but equal level,
— to establish and maintain close harmony between theory and practice. After the theoretical foundation, a practical activity has to follow, which gives sufficient motivation to adult students.
— adult students have different learning habits. But many of them continue their studies after a long break and forget the knowledge and learning habits as well. Therefore they must learn again the independent study or learning habits that suits them best.
— in connection to the above mentioned fact, the training must develop their activity, communication skills and trade skills as well.
— the continuous increasing of student's learning ability should be ensured by optimal motivation and activity.

Motivation and Learning

Motivation and learning activity create a functional unit. They are always interrelated. Learning habits depend mainly on needs, motives, interests and real attitudes. Some tasks to realise a study habit suited well to personality:

1. To motivate the student to work at the optimal level and take an active attitude towards the study process e.g.: active knowledge can be reproduced more easily than passive knowledge.
2. Achievement of activity: To set up positive goals. It is the question of long term study goals and current goals. The former enables us to get higher and longer achievement, the latter enables us only to solve a given task.
3. Relationship between the study goal and the practical professional task: The practical professional task of the study has a stronger effect on the isolated than the optimal level and takes an active attitude towards the study process. That is: active knowledge can be reproduced more easily than passive knowledge.
4. Relationship between interest and the practical professional task. The practical professional task of the study has a stronger effect on motivation than the isolated but practical examples. At best, the adult students use their own professional interests, knowledges, and experiences.
5. Situation plays, case studies give the opportunity to correct and to try different possibilities. Either the students or we create the situation. The best concept is to do them together.
6. Logical learning instead of mechanical memorisation. The most important and indispensable aspect of studying is gaining a total understanding of the subject matter, and recognising logical relationships, because adults' memory tends to shift toward intellectually organised matters.
7. Evaluation: Any learning process must have feedback about the student's achievement and his/her success. Evaluation should follow closely after finishing a given exercise because the timing progress in learning depends on the time between action and awareness of it.

8. Constant repetition and practice: Knowledge and skills should be repeated.Thus we strengthen positive behaviour and working habits. The negative habits must be eliminated of course with the assistance of the tutor, teacher.
9. The number of repetitions and their sequence depend to a great extent on the intellectual capacity of the adults and on their individual personal traits. We should strengthen successful college achievement only because it is necessary to achieve the desired effect.

So, to sum up, successful learning is only possible if the given experience and the knowledge of the adults are synthetised with the new information taught in the course. This requirement is applied to different study groups and study hours during the information flow. It means that in the teaching—learning process, the community of the students—the group—will play the main role, and not the teacher! This is a very important feature of adult education.

Skills and Values in Teacher Training

Recognising these points within the school curriculum and their broader validity, outlined below are proposed concepts, skills and values which could be perceived as a framework for global perspectives within the initial training of teachers.

Knowledge and concepts

— global dimensions of specific subjects including their historical, geographical, technical, cultural and environmental links

— interdependence of society, economy and the natural environment between the industrialised North and the South, local and global

— nature of power exercised by international institutions, corporations and finance

— awareness of global inequalities in resources and power
— nature and effects of inequalities of class, gender, race and other distinctions
— human rights, drawing on the international declaration of human rights
— citizenship and rights of democratic participation in decisions that affect people's lives
— diversity of peoples, cultures, communities, economies and points of view
— needs and rights of future generations
— quality of life, equity and justice
— sustainable change and development
— uncertainty and precaution in action

Skills

— relating participants' experience and knowledge to wider issues
— participatory learning methods
— critical analysis
— information handling and data analysis
— ability to communicate concepts, information and values in engaging ways
— working co-operatively

Values and attitudes

— responsibility for the direct and indirect impact on the world
— learning from others in the South and not assuming that the West knows best
— solidarity with people who are derided, exploited or denied human rights

— co-operation between people at a personal, local, regional and global level
— equal opportunities and social inclusion
— intercultural understanding and respect for different perspectives.

Learning Outcomes

To apply these perspectives and agendas to learning, it is proposed here that the global teacher needs to recognise three strands within the teaching and learning process:

— The desire to incorporate the local, national and international context into the formal or non-formal setting. This may be in a literacy programme through encouraging participants to use their developing skills to explore national and international issues in the media or exploring the uses of literacy in their native regions or countries.

— The emphasis placed on a set of values concerned with a commitment to interdependence; an acceptance that we are not independent either as groups or as individuals, but that our actions impact upon others, environmentally, socially, culturally and economically: democracy, social justice, perceptions and images.

— The use of a methodology which focuses on supporting active learning, valuing and building on existing knowledge, encouraging critical reflection and enabling children and young people to make informed choices in their own context.

Integrating the concepts of interdependency, social justice or a global perspective into learning outcomes for a specific course or workshop cannot just be reduced to knowledge or skills or a values base. The inclusion of a global perspective in a framework of learning does not in itself guarantee the transfer of these concepts into practice. The next stage is for these to be translated into the activities and methods that the participants or students experience in practice.

The goal therefore is for the newly qualified teacher to have the ability to apply their new skills, knowledge and values within the classroom. The challenge for teacher trainers is to look at their own courses and programmes and to consider how the global dimension can become more than just a one-off session or module, for it to become reflected across the range of teacher training provision while also making connections not only to knowledge and skills, but also to the values, attitudes and methodologies to be undertaken.

Theory in Initial Teacher Training (ITT)

Early studies of school-based ITT gave mixed messages about student teachers' evaluations of the 'new' courses. Some research suggests that trainees continue to value most highly the more 'practical', school-based elements of ITT programmes and are sceptical of the value of the (remaining or revamped) theoretical components. For example, on the evidence of a survey of student teachers on both a university-led Partnership scheme in England and an Institut Universitaire de Formation des Mai^tres (IUFM) in France, Asher and Malet state that trainees: appreciate most those elements of their courses that deal with the day-today practicalities of teaching rather than the principles that underpin them [and] ... view with greater or less degrees of antipathy those parts of the training process that may be broadly termed 'theory'.

Some other studies suggest that student teachers are now more appreciative of the Higher Education Insitutions (HEI)-based and 'theoretical' elements of ITT. For example, Holligan showed that trainees on a Primary Bachelor of Education (BEd) programme believed that 'academic studies [were] an essential component of being a professional teacher', whilst Furlong et al. note that 'learning in higher education was seen by the overwhelming majority of our respondents to have a vital role to play'. WilliamsonMcdiarmid and A. Soares offer evidence not only of high levels of trainee satisfaction with HEI-based work, but also of high levels of support amongst trainees for 'training that examines the principles behind the practice of teaching' and 'learning about how children learn'. What is not clear from many of the studies reporting student teachers' evaluations of their pre-service training is whether different student teachers have conceptualised the term 'theory' in the same way or, more fundamentally, precisely what student teachers mean and understand by the term.

Michael Eraut defines educational theory as comprising: concepts and frameworks, ideas and principles which may be used to interpret, explain or judge intentions, actions and experiences in educational or education-related settings. He also distinguishes between public and private theories, in which the former refer to 'systems of ideas' published in books, discussed in classes, etc., whilst the latter refer to ideas in people's minds that they use to interpret or explain experience, and which may be private versions of public theories.

Supporting Beginning Teachers

Beginning teacher support programmes, also referred to as teacher induction programmes, can help schools and districts meet this challenge and take advantage of the opportunity it presents. Minimally, such programmes can improve teacher retention rates by enhancing new teacher satisfaction. More importantly, a well-designed and implemented effort can improve practice, helping new educators apply the theoretical knowledge acquired in their teacher preparation programmes to the complexity of real life teaching. Not incidentally, such support programmes can also serve as a drawing card in the increasingly competitive market for hiring new teachers.

A great deal of research literature documents the extent to which beginning teachers struggle in their early classroom years. Veenman's classic international review of perceived problems among beginning teachers found remarkable consistency, across both time and differently structured education systems. Among the greatest challenges perceived by rookie teachers were classroom management, motivation of students, dealing with the individual differences among students, assessing student work, and relations with parents.

In a current international study funded by the National Science Foundation, WestEd researchers Ted Britton and Senta Raizen, along with Lynn Paine of Michigan State University, are finding that, in countries as different as China, New Zealand, and Switzerland, today's new teachers express these very same problems as being the most pressing difficulties they face. In teaching, new entrants, fresh out of professional training, assume the exact same responsibilities as 20-year veterans. In doing so, they are also undertaking a remarkably complex endeavour, involving as it does the simultaneous management of multiple variables, including student behaviour, intellectual engagement, student interaction, materials, physical space, and time.

While many novice teachers have had terrific intellectual preparation and an outstanding student teaching experience, their limited experience generally yields an equally limited repertoire of classroom strategies—far more limited than the variety of teaching challenges a new teacher invariably encounters. It's situation ripe for frustration. Not surprisingly, perhaps, the attrition rate for beginning teachers has always been extremely high, with nearly a third of novice teachers leaving the profession within their first three years.

Innercity and rural schools find it especially hard to retain teachers. This revolving door creates a permanent core of inexperienced teachers who are learning their craft by, essentially, practicing on the students before them. At the schoolwide level, high teacher turnover drains energy and resources as well, requiring that administrators and teaching colleagues constantly focus on bringing newcomers up to speed on everything from operating the copy machine to participating in major reform efforts.

When new teachers turn away from their profession, their years of teacher preparation are rendered useless, a waste both of their personal resources and of the governmental resources that subsidise such training. At the same time, of course, their departure further exacerbates existing teacher shortages. The 1980s and '90s generated a growing number of teacher induction programmes aimed at helping beginning teachers make a successful transition from their teacher preparation experience to being the teacher-of-record in a classroom.

Most such programmes identify beginning teachers as those who are either fresh out of a teacher preparation programme or who have been teaching only one or two years. But, increasingly, districts and schools recognise the need to also offer some degree of support for teachers who, while not new to the classroom per se, are new to the school, the district, or the state.

For districts or schools undertaking—or expanding—an organised support effort for beginning teachers, it helps to understand the range of strategies that have been tried in the past and what the available data, limited as they are, suggest about the effectiveness of such strategies. This general types of support that can be offered to beginning teachers, strategies of varying intensity for offering such support, institutional conditions that increase the effectiveness of these strategies, and typical challenges in the implementation of teacher induction programmes.

Beginning teacher support should be looked at as a continuum, starting with personal and emotional support, expanding to include specific task- or problem-related support and, in the ideal, expanding further to help the newcomer develop a capacity for critical self-reflection on teaching practice. Each aspect of support serves a different purpose.

Personal Support

The first years of teaching are especially stressful as beginning teachers face the emotional challenges of adapting to a new workplace and new colleagues—from simply figuring out where things are located to learning policies and procedures, finding kindred spirits, and, generally speaking, getting the lay of the land. Fatigue is another constant for new teachers. "Free" time during their official workday is scarce, and planning and other preparation invariably spills over into their personal time.

The effort of planning every lesson from scratch, teaching with unfamiliar materials, and, often, teaching at an unfamiliar grade level drains even the most energetic new teachers. Compounding all this is the inherent isolation of individual teachers sequestered in their individual classrooms.

At this emotionally challenging time, more experienced colleagues can play an important role, serving as a sounding board and assuring beginners that their experience is normal, offering sympathy and perspective, and providing advice to help reduce the inevitable stress. While this type of support does little to directly improve teaching performance, it does much to promote beginning teachers' personal and professional well-being and to transmit the culture of teaching. In the process, such support also improves the likelihood that new teachers will stay the course long enough to have the opportunity to become more effective teachers.

Problem-Focused Support

Beginning teachers also need help in knowing how to approach new tasks and in solving specific problems that crop up in their teaching. They are usually undertaking even the most basic teaching tasks for the very first time: developing lesson plans, planning what to say at back-to-school night, deciding what goes in the gradebook to determine grades at the end of nine weeks, and structuring parent-teacher conferences.

Seasoned teachers can guide beginners in planning and accomplishing these tasks effectively; with the help of a veteran teacher, the beginner doesn't have to re-invent the wheel for such standard activities. Veterans can also share the sometimes unwritten expectations associated with such tasks in a given school, district, or state.In similar fashion, attentive mentors can alert new teachers to the customs of the broader school community—everything from expectations about how quiet the corridors should be when students pass between classes to the prevailing expectations of local parents regarding parent participation in the classroom. For example, in one school, teachers might consider the faculty lounge completely off-limits to parents, while at another the lounge might double as a meeting room for parent-teacher conferences. While such conventions might not be "make-or-break" issues for new teachers, understanding them can go a long way toward making life easier.

Beginning teachers also need help in dealing with teaching challenges specific to their own students: What materials are appropriate for Maria who always finishes the assigned tasks early? What can be done to help Jeff, a special needs student, and Ming Lee, an English learner, while keeping the rest of the class productively engaged? And what can be tried when a new teacher has exhausted his or her repertoire for teaching students how to add fractions—when, for example, manipulatives, pictures, and even step-by-step instruction have achieved only limited success? By looking at such challenges from the perspective of experience or by drawing from a larger repertoire of instructional strategies and materials, veteran teachers can help beginners identify a larger range of possible solutions. This type of problem-specific support can improve teaching performance in specific instances and, as a by-product, reduce new teachers' stress levels.

Veterans' support in dealing with specific problems can help beginners expand their repertoire of strategies—from instructional delivery to classroom management to assessment—and help broaden the perspective from which newcomers view problems. But problem specific support may do little to foster rookie teachers' independent problem-solving abilities. If teachers are to become skilled at independently identifying and addressing the idiosyncratic learning problems of their students, they must learn to reflect critically on student work, as well as on their own teaching practices.

Efforts to support such self-reflection often start out with a relatively directive approach. In some instances, veteran teachers may need to help identify and then prioritise issues that warrant new teachers' reflection. Left to their own devices, novices may not even recognise the most pressing issues on which to focus their attention. For beginners who have not developed the habit of reflecting on their own teaching, the veteran may model self-reflection: identifying a problem and proposing and analysing for the beginner a variety of solutions.

In doing so, the veteran can help the beginner think in terms of being guided by evidence, for example, how will you know that your students have learned what you're trying to teach? Then, as the novice begins to develop more self-confidence and efficacy, the veteran may continue to propose solutions, but prompt the beginning teacher to analyse them himself or herself. Eventually, the beginner will be expected to autonomously propose and analyse various options for addressing a particular issue. Over time, the veteran reduces the amount of guidance offered and engages more as an interested and sympathetic colleague, shifting from a directive to collaborative to facilitative role.

The overall aim is to build beginning teachers' autonomous ability to prioritise the most challenging aspects of their teaching experience; consider alternative approaches to dealing with a given challenge; identify and analyse the evidence that provides the most information about a particular problem; and consider alternative solutions that can be quickly implemented. In the short run, beginning teachers profit by solving particular problems; but in the long run, they profit by knowing how to think constructively about any problem that comes up in their teaching.

The critical self-reflection engendered by this type of coaching can lead directly to improved teaching and learning in the beginning teacher's classroom. In the best-case scenario, such coaching can also have a broader impact, fostering in both coach and new teacher a bent toward action-oriented collegial discussion. When a critical mass of teachers at one school are comfortable talking with each other about their teaching, the school's capacity to identify and address problems in student learning and other important issues rises dramatically. This kind of dialogue allows everyone at the school to transcend the details of individual classrooms and to see the big picture of what's going on at a school or across a particular grade level. One teacher who notices that her fifth graders don't understand place value may assume the problem is idiosyncratic to her classroom. But when all the fifth grade teachers at a school come together to discuss teaching and learning in their classrooms and realise that a disproportionate number of their students don't understand place value, the school can more effectively address both the immediate problem and its causes.

Teacher Support Programmes

New-teacher support programmes may be operated by school districts or by consortia of districts, either on their own or, sometimes, in partnership or association with the local teachers association. A state department of education may also offer a beginning teacher support model, as is true of California, which provides some implementation funding as well. But schools can also do much on their own. One Nevada high school principal, who has implemented a fairly complex teacher induction programme at her school, notes, "we can do most of the things we need to do to support our new teachers with only the tacit support of the district—although it would be nice to have its active involvement."

The amount of resources schools and districts are able and willing to devote to beginning teacher support varies, of course. Some states give districts funds specifically for teacher induction programmes or for a specific type of mentor teacher programme in which mentor responsibilities focus on beginning teacher support rather than on curriculum development or special projects, for example. Often, mentor monies are used to release mentor teachers from their own classrooms part-time, but some districts have found it more effective to target the funds differently.

In California, for example, the state has given waivers that allow a district to support a smaller number of mentor teachers but have each of them work full time to support new teachers. Veteran teachers who do not have to balance both classroom and mentoring responsibilities have more time to focus on the beginning teachers, are more flexible, and, often, can respond to problems in a more timely way. Not surprisingly, the amount of available funding often affects the choice of activities that are included in a teacher induction programme. Some activities are low intensity and relatively low cost, being either one-shot or low-frequency events. As such, they require short-term but focused coordination. Others are higher intensity, tend to be costlier, require sustained attention, and, often, must be coordinated with other school or district activities.

Low-Intensity Support Strategies

Low-intensity support strategies make minimal demands on district and school resources. Some are simply procedural, such as providing formal orientation or protecting new teachers from extracurricular responsibilities. Others require the involvement of veteran teachers in mentoring or collegial roles. When veteran teachers' involvement can be structured in ways that do not impinge on their regular teaching time—in grade-level meetings, for example—districts consider such strategies to be low intensity.

Even strategies that pay stipends are considered low intensity so long as the veterans are not pulled from their classrooms. Beginning teachers, on the other hand, experience even low- intensity efforts as highly valuable when those strategies feature lots of contact with veteran teachers, contact that generally provides personal or emotional support and that helps them address the unfamiliar tasks and problems they encounter as first-time teachers.

Studies suggest that such support from veteran teachers results in higher job satisfaction and higher retention rates for beginning teachers. All of the activities below qualify as low-intensity support and can be implemented in some form by a school with little or no district involvement or funding.

— *Orienting new teachers*. The week before school, beginning teachers receive a formal orientation to the community, district, curriculum, and school. One district uses school buses to give a tour of the community, with special attention to community agencies and the neighbourhoods where students live. Orientation is also an opportunity to give an overview of curricular and school/district philosophy, share special emphases for the year, and point out important features of curriculum materials. Some districts include advice on setting up the classroom and/or classroom management. Also helpful are booklets or other handouts that document in ready form some important information, such as district policies or a calendar of key events.

— *Matching beginning and veteran teachers*. The pairing of a beginning teacher with a veteran teacher is a hallmark of most teacher induction programmes. Whether this pairing is considered to be a low- or high-intensity effort depends on the degree of support the veteran teacher is expected to provide. In low-intensity programmes, the experienced teacher is likely to function primarily as a buddy or, as one superintendent describes it, "a cheerleader," providing emotional support. In many such instances, the veteran teacher receives no release time and, therefore, doesn't have the opportunity to actually observe the new teacher

> in action. Even so, some offer enormous amounts of time and attention, often well beyond that for which they are compensated-assuming they receive any compensation at all.

Typically, novice teachers are urged to contact the veterans with any problems that arise. But some beginners are reluctant to bring problems to the attention of their support providers, either because they are embarrassed or because they don't want to be a burden, especially if novices know that the providers are receiving little or no compensation. Any type of pairing strategy is strengthened when the veteran teacher receives a stipend and the pair is expected to set aside a regular time each week to meet together. Studies suggest that without regular, structured time set aside, paired teachers have less interaction. Matching the pair by grade level or content area also increases both the likelihood of regular interaction and the effectiveness of the support.

Clarification of veteran teachers' responsibilities is important. One Arizona school district operates both a one-on-one "buddy" programme and a mentor programme. In the low-intensity buddy programme, new teachers are matched with veteran teachers whose job it is to "show them the ropes," such as how to obtain supplies or send down the lunch count. By contrast, mentors must be endorsed by their principals as "master teachers," and they are trained in specific coaching techniques. In this high-intensity programme, mentors are then matched with and receive release time to observe and work with several new teachers.

Adjusting working conditions. Unless specific administrative steps are taken to protect them, beginning teachers often end up with the toughest assignments. To make life less stressful for them, administrators can reduce the number of students in beginners' classrooms, refrain from assigning them the most challenging students, and minimise their extracurricular and committee assignments. At the elementary school level, in particular, administrators can avoid assigning combination grades. At the secondary school level, administrators can make sure that new teachers' course schedules require as few separate preparation efforts as possible. They can also avoid assigning schedules that require new teachers to change classrooms during the day. In this era of tight resources, it must also be said that beginning teachers, especially, suffer when classrooms are not adequately stocked with textbooks, desks, supplementary materials, and basic supplies.

Given the abundance of school reform efforts, a common hazard for today's beginning teachers is the sheer number of professional development activities in which they're expected to participate. At one California school, for example, beginning teachers have been expected to participate in regularly scheduled workshops aimed specifically at beginning teachers, in intensive early literacy training over several weeks, and in weekly staff-wide discussions about how to collaborate with a university in transforming their school into a professional development school. The importance of each of these specific activities notwithstanding, the demands of so many commitments can be tiring even for veteran teachers; for beginners they can be overwhelming, undermining both the effectiveness and morale of a teacher.

Principals can protect beginning teachers from getting spread too thin by helping them prioritise their time spent in professional development and by excusing them from all but the most essential activities. They can also help beginning teachers choose and focus on a single, important theme, such as literacy instruction in the example above, that might run through multiple events.

Promoting collegial collaboration. Some schools have existing structures that foster collaboration between beginning and veteran teachers, such as grade-level teams that coordinate instructional planning. Such teams provide some degree of structure and support for beginners who are just learning how to plan curriculum and instruction. For some schools, class size reduction has ended up creating another natural opportunity for ongoing collaboration between veteran and novice teachers. Rather than creating multiple classes with 20 students each, schools with limited space often respond to class-size reduction mandates by forming one class of 40 taught by two teachers. When one of those two is a veteran and the other a beginner, it's an ideal opportunity for a mentor-like relationship.

Principals can also simply ask a veteran teacher to plan together with a beginner who is teaching the same grade or the same course. At the secondary school level, this joint planning can be facilitated by common prep periods. Study groups focused on specific topics, such as using running records or improving mathematics instruction, provide beginning teachers with collaborative problem-solving models. In such groups, novices hear how veteran teachers think about using and adapting instructional techniques. It's helpful to remember that beginning teachers can also serve as important resources for a school. New teachers may well know more than veteran teachers about certain instructional approaches, having studied new techniques in their teacher preparation coursework and used them in student teaching. In certain disciplines—the sciences, for example—a new teacher may also have more current content knowledge than a colleague who has been teaching for 10 or 15 years. Here, again, collaboration profits everyone.

High-Intensity Support Strategies

Research from the California New Teacher Project, a varied set of induction programmes, indicates that high-intensity support strategies, such as those described below, are more effective than the less intensive strategies at improving beginning teaching performance. For this research, teaching performance was measured on a number of dimensions, including the complexity of academic assignments, percentage of students engaged, long-term planning of curriculum and instruction, range of instructional materials used, use of state/district guidelines and frameworks, and ability to reflect on teaching practices.

As with low-intensity efforts, here, too, veteran teachers are a key ingredient. In high-intensity support efforts, however, much more is expected of them. But if they are to operate as anything more than buddies or cheerleaders, they must be chosen carefully, receive appropriate training, and be given adequate time away from their own classroom responsibilities—all of which requires a greater commitment on the part of the school or district.

Minimally, support providers should be teachers who are successful in their own classrooms and articulate about their practice. But these are only minimum requirements. Because working with beginning teachers is different from working with children and youth, even the most outstanding K-12 teacher is not automatically suited by skill or temperament to collegial work with other adults. Regarding temperament, for example, some extremely competent teachers seem to forget how long it took them to develop into such effective practitioners. They find it difficult to appropriately downshift their expectations when working with beginning teachers who, with rare exception, cannot possibly teach as well as highly skilled 20-year veterans. Some experienced teachers, accustomed to having their students do what they ask, also find it frustrating to work with adults, who may or may not follow the guidance they offer.

However, if they are temperamentally suited to mentoring, many potential support providers can profit from training in observation skills and specific strategies for working with adults. In cognitive coaching, for example, teachers learn to initiate collegial conversations rather than combative exchanges and to support colleagues in constructing and extending their own analysis of a teaching or learning event. Support providers also benefit from training in how to collect and analyse the different types of evidence that provide insight into the degree of learning taking place in a classroom and, therefore, the effectiveness of the teaching.

Support providers must also recognise the importance of helping beginners identify and understand their teaching strengths. Beginners—and especially the more perceptive beginners—often become fixated on the areas in which they need to improve, losing sight of those things that are working well in their classrooms. Recognising and understanding their successes not only provides an enormous boost in confidence, but helps beginning teachers build on those strengths. Providing release time. Release time can be used in a number of ways to support beginning teachers.

For starters, the beginning teachers themselves can be released to attend seminars, to work with support providers to analyse their students' work and the instruction it reflects, or to observe other teachers for a specific purpose. Support providers can also be released from their own teaching duties to provide demonstration lessons in beginners' classrooms, which allows novices to see how certain techniques might be used with their own students. Veteran teachers might also use their release time to simply observe beginning teachers in action and document issues for later discussion. All of these professional development activities and more are used in New Zealand, where the national government provides funding that requires schools to provide 0.2 release time for every new teacher along with a locally developed programme to develop their abilities.

Schools with a number of beginning veteran teacher pairs sometimes use a "roving sub" who moves from classroom to classroom, releasing classroom teachers for an hour or two of focused work. Another option is for support providers to work half time with beginning teachers and half-time in classrooms they share with another teacher who wants to work only half-time. Interactive journals shared by veteran and beginner pairs can facilitate communication between them, while reducing the amount of face-to-face time they need. Veterans use the journal to document classroom observations and to raise issues for reflection and later discussion. Beginners can use it to respond in turn or to pose questions, which the veterans can then address in the journal as well. Such journals may be kept in written form in notebooks or orally, using a small tape recorder.

Common challenges of Mini-courses. Many of the issues that frustrate, stymie, or simply scare beginning teachers are predictable. Some, such as planning for back-to-school night or parent conferences, are relatively easy to address in a quick workshop. Others, such as student discipline, teaching English language learners, and assessment, are thornier and worthy of more attention.

Schools and districts can offer mini-courses or seminars during release time, after school, in the evening, or on weekends, and on their own or in partnership with universities, county offices of education, or a consortium of small districts. One Arizona district holds a five-day "rookie camp" in the week before school starts. When universities are involved, they can package a series of seminars that earn district credit or credit toward a master's degree. In fact, the same Arizona district that sponsors a rookie camp also has a partnership with the local university, which has developed its master's programme in education based, in part, on the content needed by district teachers.

Mini-courses and seminars are most effective when beginning teachers receive support in applying the knowledge learned. Opportunities for relevant role play can be built into the course. Participants can also develop action plans for applying their new knowledge, and those plans can then be critiqued by their classmates. If support providers also attend the mini-course or are informed of its contents, they can then provide relevant support as beginners start applying what they have learned.

Veteran teachers can help beginners collect evidence of their teaching practice and analyse it to identify both strengths and areas for improvement. This strategy is most effective when the veteran and beginner pairs take a particular focus, either on a classroom problem or perhaps on competencies the beginner is expected to exhibit. Evidence may come from a veteran's observations of a beginner's interactions with his or her own students, from joint analysis of student work, or even from an examination of the arrangement of classroom materials and furniture. Universities can often provide training or expertise in collecting and interpreting evidence, such as through observation or portfolio documentation. In some instances, universities collaborate with districts by actually conducting the observations to provide evidence. Often, an examination of evidence results in a professional development plan for the beginning teacher, with activities targeted to specific areas of growth.

Teaching standards adopted by a state or district identify expected competencies, although rarely at a beginning level. As an articulation of what experienced teachers should know and be able to do, such standards alone are not especially helpful for the novice. However, the Interstate New Teacher Assessment and Support Consortium publishes a model set of standards that are widely used by teacher preparation programmes. These standards are intended to serve as a basis for discussion and adaptation by states, but can also be adapted to district needs.

Now being piloted in that state, goes further, providing rubrics, or performance levels, for each competency. These rubrics can help the beginner and the veteran interpret the evidence they collect regarding the beginner's own practices. The rubrics also provide solid ideas about what's reasonable to expect for the teacher's next stage of development. In setting goals for the beginning teacher, it's important that they be challenging, but also attainable. Teacher assessment instruments, such as the California Teaching Portfolio, developed by WestEd, or Pathwise, developed by the Educational Testing Service, also have rubrics built into them.

Institutional Policies and Practices

Certain institutional policies and practices strengthen all beginning teacher support efforts—starting with having an effective method for identifying new teachers and maintaining realistic expectations for these newcomers.

Early identification of beginning teachers by the personnel office. Few personnel offices are set up to formally identify new teachers (whether new to the profession, the state, or the district) and provide that information to their principals or to the coordinator of an induction programme. Early identification does, however, aid in planning for specific support activities, such as orientation. It also allows support to begin much earlier in the year.

Realistic expectations for beginners. It takes time for teachers to learn their craft. Induction programmes can accelerate beginning teacher growth, but most newcomers will still need an extended period before they look like strong veteran teachers. Yet most teacher evaluation systems do not distinguish between beginning and veteran teachers. No one wants to see incompetent teachers in classrooms, but in this era of rising expectations, care must be taken that beginning teachers are not continually hired and then let go in the name of raising standards. Sustained investment of support in beginning teachers who are consistently improving their teaching is a wise policy, especially for districts that are at a disadvantage in hiring teachers.

Cooperative agreements with unions. While teacher unions and associations are generally supportive of teacher induction practices, they are wary of setting any undesirable precedents. For example, because issues related to compensation for time spent in required activities are important to all teachers, teacher representatives may also want to negotiate clear limits to the amount of uncompensated time contributed by veteran teachers and beginning teachers in the course of a support programme. They are also typically interested in how support providers are selected, especially if a stipend is involved. Having union representatives participate in the planning of support programmes or discussion of particularly thorny issues ahead of time can help avoid grievances and divisive struggles.

Coordination of efforts. Even when adopting low-intensity support strategies, a district or school needs someone who is paying attention to implementation, dealing with obstacles, and ensuring consistency with other district policies. Whether considering beginning teacher orientations, seminars, coursework, or even pairing beginners with veteran teachers, someone with administrative authority must lay the groundwork. Dates and facilities must be scheduled to avoid conflicts with other school and district activities. Veteran teachers who are willing to work with beginners must be identified, recruited, and trained.

Both support and training for these mentors must be ongoing. If the support strategies for beginning teachers are planned at a district level, someone needs to ensure that principals are aware of the nature, timing, and purpose of the various activities. Experience suggests that this is unlikely to happen unless the person responsible for doing all this also has a realistic amount of time set aside for it. Release time. Protected time makes it more likely that classroom observations will take place, that veterans and beginners will actually meet and have discussions that are not rushed, and that beginners will attend seminars at times when fatigue does not interfere with their ability to pay attention. The creative use of substitutes and staff development days can enhance the effectiveness of support activities.

Challenges for Support Programmes

Like beginning teachers themselves, teacher induction programmes face some predictable challenges. These include identifying and preparing support providers, providing time for support activities, managing the relationship between support and evaluation, and securing resources for struggling teachers. Choosing and preparing support providers. Finding teachers to serve as support providers is a constant challenge, especially if few incentives are available and support is provided by volunteers. Even when stipends are available, the dollars are rarely commensurate with the amount of time required.One California induction programme attempts to generate future support providers by asking beginners to identify teachers other than their support providers who were helpful; these supportive teachers then receive certificates of appreciation along with information about becoming an official support provider. A school or district can also identify potential support providers by soliciting nominations from principals, staff developers, and teachers. Larger districts may create full-time positions for support providers, although this is expensive unless subsidised by state or federal entitlement funds or by a special grant solicited specifically to fund new teacher support. The selection process is further complicated by the fact that, as noted earlier, excellent classroom teachers do not always make the best support providers for beginning teachers. In districts and schools with few opportunities for teachers to work collegially, it may be difficult to predict who has the temperament and skills to work with beginners. Another selection challenge is the uneven distribution of effective support providers across schools. Meetings between beginners and support providers are more effective when the paired teachers teach at the same grade level or in the same content area, and the meetings generally occur with greater frequency when the paired teachers are at the same school.

Typically, there is not enough time to provide all the preparation that might be desirable, so induction programmes are forced to concentrate on the training believed to be most important. Some programmes focus preparation on coaching skills; others focus on collecting and interpreting evidence of teaching. The most extensive preparation does both. The issue is further complicated if the induction programme is expected to address a set of teaching standards, as in the California Beginning Teacher Support and Assessment Programme. In that case, support providers must become familiar with the teaching standards. Occasionally, a district finds a way to make a real financial commitment to new-teacher support. Another Arizona district has solved the "find and prepare" problem by maintaining a cadre of carefully trained master teachers, known as Instructional Programme Specialists. These are classroom teachers employed on teacher contracts but deployed on "special assignment," a significant portion of which is to support new teachers through a three-year formal mentoring relationship. These specialists work directly with new teachers in their classrooms, assessing their practice and doing demonstration teaching. Their basic training covers clinical supervision, cognitive coaching, group facilitation strategies, cooperative learning, essential elements of instruction, classroom management strategies, multiple intelligences, and district curriculum standards, as well as training in various software programmes aligned with district curriculum. In addition, they receive ongoing training as the curriculum is revised and new instructional materials are adopted for student use.

Every education reform effort struggles with the issue of time. Every support activity is more likely to happen if time is provided during regular working hours or if teachers are paid for attendance. However, this imposes a tremendous logistical and financial burden on teacher induction programmes. Programmes manage this challenge by reserving time within the school day or with paid time for the activities deemed most important. Beginning teachers are especially busy, since they typically spend nights and weekends planning lessons. So any after-school support activities further cut into the time left for any personal life. In addition, beginning teachers need time to think about their teaching in order to grow in their craft.

Induction programmes must make sure that beginners' time is not filled with formal activities that have little relationship to their teaching, that leave little room for their immediate concerns, or that deny them a reasonable personal life. Managing the relationship between beginning teacher support and beginning teacher evaluation. Beginning teacher support programmes focus on improving practice. In contrast, evaluation programmes focus on comparing a teacher's practice to a standard that must be met if beginners are to keep their jobs. Many believe that in fairness to new teachers, the two efforts must be kept entirely separate. Naturally, this separation precludes the principal, who is the teachers' primary evaluator, from participating closely in support efforts.

A few induction programmes have successfully combined the support and evaluation of beginning teachers. These programmes provide high levels of intensive support to beginning teachers in areas that have been clearly identified to them as requiring growth. Most induction programmes, however, separate support and evaluation, due either to a belief that evaluation interferes with support or to concerns about losing union support. In keeping support and evaluation separate, confidentiality is a critical issue, requiring explicit understanding about what support providers will or will not share with principals.

In programmes that separate support and evaluation, support providers can usually respond to principals' request to target assistance in a particular area, but they do not report on the perceived success of that effort. Some induction programmes ask support providers and beginning teachers to keep the principal informed of general areas in which they are working, such as classroom management or lesson planning. However, when it comes to providing specific information about a beginner's practice to anyone conducting an evaluation, the mentor must refuse. And in keeping such information confidential, they must be supported by district administrators.

Whatever a school's rules about confidentiality related to teacher support, if a beginning teacher and support provider are to work together effectively, the new teacher must trust the intentions of the provider. For that reason, the beginning teacher, the support provider, and the principal must all have the same understanding of those rules from the outset. Another area for concern relates to aligning evaluation criteria—those used by support providers to help beginning teachers improve and those used by school administrators to evaluate beginners for retention. The criteria should be the same for both purposes. Such alignment helps avoid the kind of awkward situations—and potential lawsuits—that can come about when beginning teachers receive contradictory feedback from support providers and evaluators.

Both support providers and school administrators evaluating beginners should receive training aimed at developing shared understandings about the minimum criteria and standards beginners must meet as a condition of continued employment. Getting resources to struggling teachers. While many beginners will perform adequately even with minimal assistance, some will struggle. These teachers require more support than that provided in most low-intensity strategies; in fact, even programmes using high intensity strategies will need to determine how to strategically focus support. Ideally, programmes can be flexibly designed to allow some resources to be shifted from beginners who are doing fine to those who are not.

7

Modern Strategies of PE Teacher Training

The primary aims of physical education vary historically, based on the needs of the time and place. Often, many different types of physical education occur simultaneously, some intentionally and others not. Most modern school systems claim their intent is to equip students with the knowledge, skills, capacities, and values along with the enthusiasm to maintain a healthy lifestyle into adulthood. Some schools also require physical education as a way to promote weight loss in students. Activities included in the program are designed to promote physical fitness, to develop motor skills, to instill knowledge and understanding of rules, concepts, and strategies, and to teach students to work as part of a team, or as individuals, in a wide variety of competitive activities.

The role of teacher is sought to be determined during the recent decades, not only in the context of providing the dimension of values in our system of education but also in the context of providing more effective methods of education. These two contexts are not mutually exclusive, and they tend to lead to conclusions that converge upon the important point, namely that the role of the teacher is not merely that of a lecturer. The International Commission on the Development of Education, established by UNESCO, submitted its report in 1972 under the title: *Learning To Be*. In this report, certain far-reaching recommendations have been made in regard to teachers and teachers' training programme. It has been, for example, pointed out: "One of the essential tasks of educators at present is to change the mentalities and qualifications inherent in all professions; thus they should be the first to be ready to rethink and change the criteria and basic situation of the teaching profession, in which the job of educating and simulating students is steadily superseding that of simply giving instructions."

It has been further pointed out that the present day divisions between formal and informal, school and out-of-school, child and adult education are steadily fading. It has, therefore, been recommended that the conditions in which teachers are trained should be profoundly changed so that, essentially, they become educators rather than mere specialists in transmitting pre-established curricula. It has been underlined that the teaching profession will not be in a position to fulfil its role in the future unless it is given, and develops itself, a structure better adapted to modern educational systems.

Widespread and efficient use of new technologies in education is possible only if sufficient change takes place within the system itself. It has, therefore, been recommended that teacher training programmes should be so modified that teachers are equipped for the different roles and functions imposed by new technologies.

The qualities, capacities and skills that we should aim at among teachers should include:

(a) A spontaneous but well-cultivated interest in observing students with deep insight and sympathy;

(b) Psychological tact to deal with collective and individual needs of growth of students;

(c) Capacity to lead students to the art of self-learning;

(d) A cheerful and enthusiastic disposition capable of inspiring students to pursue values and excellence with sincerity and dedication;

(e) Capacity of guiding and counselling, more by suggesting and by uplifting example rather than by lecturing;

(f) Capacities not only for a formal education but also for non-formal and informal education;

(g) Capacity to handle self-learning equipment, audio-visual instruments and various kinds of new learning materials including work sheets, workbooks, programmed books, test papers with auto-correcting components and other materials required for vocational guidance;

(h) Knowledge of art and science of educating the personality in all its aspects with a special emphasis on integration, harmony and excellence.

As a practical measure, the methods which are currently employed in the teachers' training institutions should be so changed that the trainees would have the opportunity of first hand experience of new methods and techniques of learning during their training programmes. A working model that could be suggested may be described as follows:

(a) Teachers under training should at the outset be provided with a document explaining the new roles for the teachers as also various new methods and techniques involved in the learning-teaching process.

(b) Trainees would be required to indicate their willingness to employ new methods of learning in their own training;

(c) Trainees would then be advised to study their various subjects, as far as possible, through the process of self-learning;

(d) Educators of the trainees would be available for consultation as and when needed, for shorter or longer duration, by prior appointment, or at certain hours of the day, without any prior appointment;

(e) Educators would deliver lectures from time to time, as and when necessary, but these lectures would be much fewer than in the ordinary system of education;

(f) Educators would combine lectures with seminars, tutorials, demonstrations, exhibitions and individualised guidance so as to make the process of training as effective as possible;

(g) Each trainee would undertake a project, the report of which would, at the end of the training period, indicate his pursuit of excellence and values which are sought to be promoted through the training programme;

(h) The training institution should provide opportunities and facilities to the trainees to handle audio-visual equipment, new learning-teaching material, work sheets, programmed books, teaching machines and other latest instruments meant for individualised learning as also for various other methods which are sought to be employed in new emerging models of teaching-learning;

(i) Educators in the training institutions would devote themselves to extending to the trainees the necessary help, guidance, counsel and inspiration;

(j) Education would give to the trainees individualised tests from time to time, as and when necessary, with a view to giving opportunities to the trainees:

- (a) to revise what they have studied;
- (b) to ascertain the degree of proficiency achieved;
- (c) to stimulate and encourage them to study further; and
- (d) to develop new interest and new lines of studies;

(k) A record of progress would be maintained by each trainee in which he will record, among other things, books read and results achieved at various tests.

In order that the candidate is free to direct his own training programme he should be free to take or not to take any particular test during the training programme, except when in the view of the educators he is unable to use his freedom intelligently and prudently and is therefore in need of compulsory compliance with the advise and directions of the educators.

At the end of the training period, the candidates would have the possibility of taking a Public Examination, provided that he obtains from the head of the training institution a testimonial that he has shown during the training period qualities of regularity, punctuality and diligence in work as also disciplined behaviour.

— The Public Examination should consist of a written test and an oral test.

— The written test will consist of at least four papers. Of these, one paper will cover the programme that has been suggested as the core programme of value-oriented education.

— The second paper would pertain to achievements of Indian Culture, National struggle for freedom, ideals of Liberty, Equality an Fraternity, and the theme of Unity of Mankind.

— The next two papers would pertain to any combination of subjects that the student might have chosen to specialise in.

In the oral test, each interviewee would have the opportunity to explain the report of the project that he might have submitted earlier, on completion of the training period. In addition, the interviewee will be tested in respect of the depth of knowledge of subjects of his specialisation as also in respect of the general attainments of the development of personality and dedication of serious thought and to high ideals. The interview should be of a duration of at least half an hour.

One of the serious maladies of the written tests is that of cheating practised by a number of students. Various suggestions have been made to cure this malady. Some suggestion to arrange the written tests are listed below:

(a) There should be a question bank in every concerned library where a number of questions pertaining to various topics of studies could be available.

(b) Students should be free to get themselves acquainted with the questions pertaining to their own subjects and topics.

(c) In the examination hall, a selection from the totality of these questions, classified subject-wise (and topic-wise, if necessary) should be available.

(d) These questions would be printed on a specially designed paper, each question on a separate slip on one side only. The other side of the slip would be blank and slip would be so folded that only the blank side would be visible from outside.

(e) Each student would be permitted to pick up any questions by lot, and he would be expected to answer any four or five of these questions.

(f) For every question, there would be separate answer sheet, and at the commencement of the answer, the student would be required to paste the question slip.

(g) Thus, every student will have a separate set of questions, and there would be no possibility of leakage or of cheating.

Candidates who would be declared successful at this Public Examination would be entitled to appointment, on a competitive basis, to a teaching post in any secondary school. He will similarly be entitled to appointment in any higher secondary school, provided that he has the requisite post-graduate qualification as well.

ICTs in Teacher Training

The most obvious technique for professional development for teachers is to provide courses in basic ICTs knowledge and skills, delivered by experts in national and regional centres. These types of courses, taught at training centres or universities with a syllabus set by regional or national agencies, have been a common practice in many countries. However, this approach has had limited success without follow-on training and support, as compared to effective use of ICTs by trained teachers. Similarly, courses for teachers in particular software and hardware applications are difficult to implement in a way that results in use of these applications in classroom instruction or other professional practices without additional support. The development of ICTs does not improve education if the focus is on ICTs. The vision must focus on what ICTs can do to improve education.

Over the last decade, many countries that included ICTs in education were slow to also include it in teacher education. Only recently have national agencies begun to realise the importance of educating teachers at the beginning of their careers. Younger people are more likely to be familiar with ICTs, to be adaptable, and to not yet have formed habitual modes of instruction that are more difficult to change with more experienced teachers. It is in the pre-service stage that they are most open to learning how to infuse technology into instruction. Based on their long experiences with traditional modes of learning, teacher educators may find it challenging to incorporate ICTs into their own instructional practices. They may also lack experience in developing the com-plex partnerships between higher education and schools that facilitate technology-rich contexts for training student teachers. To bring this about, it is usually necessary that the faculty be held accountable to standards and that the institution provides both incentives and resources to support technology-rich programmes and initiatives.

One approach that encourages collaboration between the teacher preparation programme and the community is the formation of computer clubs for students interested in computers and education. This approach was used successfully in Russia and works well where computing resources are limited. Care must be taken, however to ensure that the emphasis is on education rather than on games or competitions. Peer tutoring models are very effective in club settings and may develop into reciprocal mentoring with teachers in which the students provide ICT training for peers and teachers and the teachers mentor the tutors' developing skills as teachers. Peer tutoring is a relatively common approach in classrooms of cultures around the world. This approach is effective even when teachers have little ICT skill and knowledge. Parents and other community members may also serve as teachers, tutors, and co-learners, and the whole community may benefit economically because of an increase in the ICT skills among diverse members of the community. GenY is a peer tutoring approach that has been successful in many places, including the Caribbean and the USA.

ICTs may also support effective professional development of teachers in to how to use ICTs. A limited initiative to integrate an innovative approach to teaching and learning with one new technology for a large population of teachers can be an important early step for a nationwide strategy. The UNESCO document, Teacher Education Through Distance Learning describes interactive radio, a professional development model in which radio programmes provide daily half-hour lessons introducing pupils to English through active learning experiences with native English speakers. The radio programmes reach 11,000 teachers across South Africa. The initiative is successful in developing teachers' pedagogical, language, and technology skills. Much of this success is due to the appropriateness of the technology choice for South Africa.

When ICTs are introduced into a community, they may address multiple goals and may expand our conception of education. For example, the Drik project in Bangladesh started as an ecology project. The goal was to plant trees and educate the local population in how to care for them. The project brought a single computer with an Internet link into the community. The introduction of this computer, coupled with peer tutoring, resulted in the development of considerable ICT skills in the young people of the region, and today the school is a centre for ICT services both locally and globally (including the USA). Although the teachers were not the leaders in this initiative, they learned to adopt ICTs and incorporate them into the curriculum and administration of their school. This extension of the 'business' of the school beyond traditional education tasks is not unusual for schools in economically depressed communities that learn the value of technology in enhancing vocational opportunities.

MirandaNet is an important example of teachers who use ICTs to mentor each other and to establish new communities connected through the Internet. The brainchild of an active teacher educator and consultant, MirandaNet is supported by partners in business and commerce. Originating in the UK, MirandaNet has spawned related communities in the Czech Republic and Chile, and negotiations are underway for a Chinese MirandaNet.

Integrating ICT into Teaching

In an effort to implement ICT standards in a variety of coursework taken by preservice teachers across all subject disciplines, a number of methods and strategies have been identified. Many of these strategies employ commonly used productivity tools such as word processing, database, spreadsheet, or browser applications. These software tools can be used in countless ways to support the subject area curricula.

Web-Based Lessons

A WebQuest is an inquiry-oriented activity in which most or all of the information used by learners is drawn from the Web. WebQuests are designed to use learners' time well, to focus on using information rather than looking for it, and to support learners' thinking at the levels of analysis, synthesis, and evaluation. The WebQuest model has been effectively applied to all levels of education, from elementary to postgraduate study, and in many different subject Areas. The WebQuest provides teachers an option of reviewing and selecting web-based learning activities in a lesson type format.The WebQuest model encourages teachers to create for their students new activities and adapt successful ones to take advantage of the Web's power. A higher-level application of this model has students develop their own Web-Quest activities to support the subject matter they are studying, and share the WebQuests with their peers.

CyberGuides

CyberGuides include standards-based, web-delivered units of instruction centred on core works of literature. CyberGuides provide a quick supplementary set of activities for students (and pre-service teachers) as they explore specific pieces of literature. Each CyberGuide contains a student and teacher edition, targeted standards, a description of the task, a process by which the task may be completed, teacher-selected web sites, and an assessment rubric. The teacher's guide includes an overview of the activities, suggestions from the author, and a library of links. The student guides include activity directions written in a format appropriate for the age and reading ability of the students.

Multimedia Presentations

Multimedia combines media objects such as text, graphics, video, animation, and sound to represent and convey information. In this project-based method of teaching and learning, students acquire new knowledge and skills by designing, planning, and producing a multimedia product. Many teachers find that students are motivated to learn when they can use technology to present the results of a rich project or activity. The multimedia presentation contains content conveyed by the student's selection of media. The teachers in training can look at examples of projects and lessons, at Internet sites housing collections of student samples. Some examples of multimedia presentations include:

— creating a web page or site;
— developing a branching hypermedia stack;
— using a multimedia slide show application to create a computer presentation;
— shooting and editing video to create a computer-generated movie.

As new forms of multimedia are explored, the types of projects become more complex. Multimedia-authoring tools are used to link and branch screens, making them interactive and layered with information in photos, scanned images, movies, and text. Students and candidates can easily narrate their projects using a microphone.

Telecomputing Projects

Telecomputing projects are Internet-enriched learning activities that often involve students in one location collaborating with students or adults in one or more other locations. They may share, among other things:

— experiences
— beliefs
— data
— information
— problem-solving strategies
— products they have developed or jointly developed.

Telecomputing tools include email, electronic mailing lists, electronic bulletin boards, discussion groups, web browsers, real-time chatting, and audio- and video-conferencing. Online resources include web sites, interactive environments, and remotely operated robotic devices.

Online Discussions

A common type of telecomputing activity is online discussion. With the growth of infrastructure around the world comes the ability to access others through remote connections. Students and teacher candidates can connect to experts and peers through a variety of formats, such as chat rooms, electronic bulletin boards, and email. Communicating online offers participants freedom to send and receive information efficiently across diverse geographic locations.

Communication can occur asynchronously allowing time for reflection, or to compensate for varying time zones. In real-time online communication, as in chat groups, the communication is synchronous and provides immediate feedback for reinforcement and understanding. Examples of online environments include email lists and virtual meeting places such as Tapped In. Tools such as Blackboard, and WebCT may be used to create online environments. Particular care should be taken when planning these activities across cultures and languages. Online discussions can provide rich learning experiences as the inter-cultural exchanges develop both linguistic skills and cultural knowl-edge. One successful strategy is for students to read in the target language, while writing in their native language.

The Three Pomegranate Network of Armenian provides an excellent example of connecting a society in Diaspora-almost two thirds of Armenians live outside their contemporary homeland. The project links different Armenian schools across the world, each with varying degrees of access to technology and training, but all wishing to strengthen their awareness of a shared personal heritage, including the Armenian language and alphabet.

The ICT curriculum for Armenian teachers is project-based and structured around a task, such as the production of a web-based newsletter. The project provides valuable strategies for the planning of curriculum across cultures and schools, which are summarised as follows:

— *Language*: Instructions and other input from the project designers are bilingual. Students work in the target language, Armenian in this case. Software has been developed to include the target language alphabet.

— *Points of contact*: Schools serving Armenian children are linked electronically to schools in Armenia in the collaborative projects. Home and community centres need careful development to act as coordinating centres for curriculum projects.

— *Informal catalyst*: An informal catalyst to collaboration is necessary. In this project, the school in Armenia always takes this role.

— *Community building*: the projects, exercise and games are specially designed for the Diaspora, including activities that introduce students new to their culture.

— *Connectivity*: The project uses a flexible set of connectivity solutions including: direct access, connectivity centres, the Web, and CD's as a means of providing wider access.

They further give guidance in setting up such a network, emphasising the important role of ICT teacher educators and leaders. There is a significant need for highly committed project managers to shepherd the project through its various stages. These stages include web and learning-activity design, identifying participants from a worldwide audience, and overcoming many logistical issues associated with adding content to a school curriculum and identifying Internet resources.

ICTs and New Approaches to Teaching

The challenge confronting countries, regions and universities is to address the following basic principles for ICTs in teacher education:

— ICTs should be infused into the entire teacher education programme.

— Technology should be introduced in context.

— Students should experience innovative ICT-supported learning environments in their teacher education programme.

The most critical factor in the successful integration of ICTs into teacher education is the extent to which the teacher educators have the knowledge and skills for modelling the use of ICTs in their own teaching practices. To enable them to develop these skills requires a well-conceived and sustained programme of professional development.

Countries that have initiated efforts to infuse ICTs into teacher education have found four professional development strategies helpful in successful technology integration. First, professional development needs to focus on teaching and learning rather than on hardware and software. It should be designed by first considering what student teachers are expected to know and be able to do in a specific discipline, and then infusing ICTs into the learning process so that acquiring the knowledge and skills is more efficient.

Second, professional development is practically useless unless leaders and teacher educators are provided with access to technology resources and have the time and support-when needed—to apply the new knowledge and skills that they have learned. A just-in-time approach to professional development is a model that works well. In this approach, professional development is provided to teacher educators when they have a need or opportunity to use a specific technology tool or application to enhance learning.

Third, professional development in the use of ICTs is not a one-time activity. To keep current with new developments means that professional development in ICTs must be an ongoing process.

A further strategy for professional development is to start in a small way. Start by providing professional development in the use of ICTs to a small group of teaching staff. Perhaps this group will have volunteered or demonstrated that they have basic ICT competencies for personal use, or have expressed personal interest in using ICTs in their teaching. Working with this small group allows the professional development staff to determine the specific interests and needs of the teacher educators and what works best in the professional development process. Based on this experience, professional development may be provided to other small groups of faculty, thus expanding and refining the professional development efforts.

The most important criterion for effective professional development is to tailor it to the learning needs and skill levels of individual teaching staff within a faculty. This suggests that, ideally, an institution should, based on availability of resources, provide a variety of options for professional development for the faculty. In structuring professional development options and resources, it is helpful to explore collaboration opportunities with partners outside the university. The opportunities for ICTs to create new paradigms of teaching and learning will depend largely on leadership and a shared vision, and on appropriate and continuing professional development.

The planning and implementation of ICT-related professional development of teacher educators should be led by a planning group that includes representation and expertise from teacher educators, programme administrators, teachers, school administrators, technology experts, and business leaders. The diverse perspectives of the group should provide an understanding of the realities of the classroom, new views of the teaching-learning process, knowledge of the array of technologies that may be used to enhance learning, and community opinions. It is important for a planning group to negotiate a shared understanding of the role of ICTs in the agenda for educational renewal based on their individual cares and concerns. It is also helpful to have a larger advisory or liaison group that may facilitate collaborative professional development efforts and sharing of resources across related organisations, for example, between the university and the partner schools where students are placed for teaching practice.

An important aspect of professional development is not only enabling teacher educators to understand and use ICT tools in their teaching practices, but understanding how technology coupled with new approaches to teaching and learning, may enhance student learning. Many teacher educators recognise that approaches to education are changing and that new technology has the potential to improve education and student learning. They may also recognise the implications of increasing use of technology in society and employment, including employment directly related to their own disciplines and content areas. Less obvious are the implications for literacy and numeracy at the core of the educational process, and the need for teacher educators themselves to model good practice in their teaching so that their students can easily transfer these strategies into their own teaching practice. Teacher educators are experts in a domain, and it is important to respect this domain while helping them to revitalise and modernise their teaching with ICTs.

The most significant change required of individuals and organisations providing teacher education is to redefine student roles and responsibilities. This is referred to as student-centred learning, and in the context of teacher education means that control of the teachingleaning process must move away from the teacher educator to the student of teaching. Both students and teachers have always had rights and responsibilities, but the redefinition of the learning environment requires a change in the balance of rights and responsibilities, with the student assuming more of both. ICTs demand this shift because technologies are constantly changing. Students need to develop the ability to think for themselves, continually learn as technologies change, and provide support to one another. This last element, peer teaching, is a natural product of ICTs because often the younger generations bring increasingly high levels of competence into the learning environment. This is a positive shift, and it should be noted that these strategies (learning from peer support and reciprocal mentoring between teacher and learner) are also appropriate for competencies that do not involve ICTs.

Professional Development

Teachers and teacher educators develop ICT competence in stages. Those who are fluent with technology may not appreciate how difficult it is for technology novices to appropriate ICTs into their professional practice. Teacher educators often find this task even more difficult than teachers do, because they typically have higher levels of content and pedagogical expertise that must be respected. Teacher educators, because they have to work in multiple contexts—both the home institution and the field where students are placed to observe and practice teaching—may also be more influenced by the absence of the essential conditions for ICTs in teacher education.

Four stages are common, but they may be repeated with new forms of ICTs or applications of ICTs to new areas. The first stage for each individual is awareness, and the appropriate response at this stage is to provide information about a relevant application of ICTs and appropriate ways that it may be used in the individual's current professional or personal concerns. Please note the learner-centred nature of this approach; the concerns are not those of the supporter or the organisation, but of the individual teacher educator. Teacher educators then explore the use of the application. They need support to put this ICT application into practice in a timely manner and to reflect on its effectiveness. Only after teacher educators have gone through these stages are they able to adapt their practice to make better use of ICTs, and then move toward the final stage to become innovators and modellers of excellent practice for their students and colleagues.

The advent of ICTs provides the opportunity to engage in this process from a new perspective and to model processes of learning for colleagues and students. It is acceptable for teacher educators to adopt only those aspects of ICTs that are relevant to their practice, but they must first be allowed to explore the range of possibilities, so that they and their students may become critically aware of, and competent in, diverse ICT applications. Of course, any teacher educators continually strive to be responsive to developments and innovations in education within and beyond their discipline.

Challenges of Teachers

Consideration of the teacher's role becomes somewhat abstract in the background of the unpleasant reality that although there is in our country a large army of teachers and a sizeable number and variety of institutions for professional training of the teachers, there is no "profession' of teaching as such indicative of what the teachers stand for and what responsibility the profession professes to own for itself. It spite of more than three decades of independence, the authoritarian control, characteristic of the sad imperial times, still prevails and the teacher is told what he must do and how to do what he must. He is not expected to have a mind of his own and he is only marginally involved, if at all, in decision making relating to goals, means administration and organisation of education all of which is done for him by others and done remotely.

The teacher is expected merely to obey; teach what he is asked to teach; teach those pupils in the selection of whom he has had little choice; limit his teaching to the books and courses prescribed; train pupils in his charge to pass examinations which are held and evaluated by others and finally be judged and rewarded by standards which have hardly any concern with his professional conscience. His task is more or less mechanical and he must carry out instructions conveyed to him by the grand machinery of education consisting of boards of education, universities, government departments and others.

Professional idealism, professional morality, professional conscience, professional standards of behaviour and, in brief, the professional spirit, does not grow in vacuum of professional responsibility and involvement in relevant decision-making relating to education. It would sound cruel but it is not for wrong to say that the teachers constitute only a large labour force for building education as best technicians and mechanics but not builders, designers and architects. This would be evident from the major concerns expressed by our teachers' organisations and associations, which are not unlike those of other labour organisations in respect of manner of expression which is not invariably elegant and dignified as well as of substance of demands which hardly goes beyond the size of the pay packets and personal benefit. It is sometimes asked, would it matter to education at all, if professional training such as is imparted at present to the various categories of teachers is withdrawn? It would not be pure cynicism to answer that some good money will be saved and education will be spared much unmerited damage that is being done to it by the formality of training required only to meet the regulations governing selection of professional staff.

The freedom allowed by the states to the higher echelons of the teaching profession, which are excused formal profession education, has also not been used for cultivation of professional spirit nor the imperative need of the present time in our country is to create conditions necessary for cultivation of refined professional personality and life-style for the teacher worthy of his responsibility and dignity as an inspirer, and, to no small extent, as a fashioner of the human destiny. Teacher is too low nor too high in the hierarchy of the profession to be denied the elevating experience.

The image of the teacher varies from time to time, country and cultural traditions of different races and seems to be influenced to no small extent by the prevailing conditions and problems of life, vital to the individual and the community. Expectations from the teacher differ and even conflict. Sparta, of old, was intolerant of the weaklings who were better left to perish unlamented; only the strong and able were to be made stronger and abler. This attitude contracts with the distrust of talent expressed by the unimaginative devotees of democracy as well as, on the other extreme, with the contemporary human concern for the mentally and physically handicapped.

We still entertain administration for some of the stern but genuinely good hearted teachers who believed that education was best imparted through the rod, the neglect of which was equated with unbecoming softness and professional irresponsibility. This picture differs widely from some of the contemporary permissive attitudes which encourage primrose-pathing and even dalliance and suffer anarchical out-bursts and destructive actions of the pupils as legitimate expression of protest against the failings of the ruling generation.

In our own country, we cherish nostalgically the idyllic picture of the ashrams of our "rishis" located in secluded forests, "far from the madding crowds ignoble strife," where the teacher and the taught shared, alike, the chores of life as well as lofty philosophy. To live in the ashrams, the wallless institutions; to live with nature and to sit at the feet of the master and watch him live and work and think was considered to be the best of education.

Behind the seeming differences in the role of the teacher in various societies, some common attitudes are discernible. One such feature relates to the culture of the people which the teacher is expected to communicate to the new generation along with its hopes and fears. In open societies with liberal traditions, culture is not forced down the throats of the pupils.

The teacher is free to interpret culture and its significance to the contemporary problems of life and to allow criticism by students of its various aspects and implications. The pupils are not expected to accept cultural attitudes of the past as a creed but they have to be aware of the ripe thinking of the past generations on problems which have mattered to life of the people and to its happiness. In other societies where the needs of education are confined to the ends of the state, the options for the teacher are restricted and he is expected to be a conformist and to indicate in the minds of the pupils dogmatic acceptance of political ideologies for theological doctrines advocated by the leadership in power.

There are also societies which have recently recovered freedom after long periods of political and cultural domination where there is a kind ambivalence because of cultural alienation. Unsure of their identify, the people tend to be eclectic and view their problems as outsiders would view them, that is, with little emotion and sense of involvement. It takes time to get over the mental attitudes to which people get accustomed through generations of educational and cultural influences and it requires no small courage to look at things afresh. Even if it means mounting a big effort, it is necessary that the process of self-examination and self-determination which are essential to all cultures, should begin and continue vigorously.

There are teachers and teachers. Socrates crusaded against the sophists of his time who taught the youth to be clever and to learn effective rhetoric to gain popular applause by making the worse appear the better reason.. Fagin, character of Dickens, taught small urchins the fine art of pick pocketing. We have teachers who teach wrestling, cricket, judo, karate and other sports. We also have teachers who teach music, painting, manual skills, workshop practice, agricultural operations and other arts and crafts necessary for making money and earning a livelihood.

But the working 'teachers' do not refer to those who train pupils merely for making a living—not as it is sometimes said for "preparing slaves to a machine or to an office or to a single money making skill." It is true that a teacher with a vision can give liberal orientation to instruction in any special skill or vocation. The word teacher, however, refers to those who impart education fitted for a free man, free to order his life according to his well-conceived thoughts and philosophy of life, free from whatever social and other pressure which inhibit or compel the mind of man.

Education for freedom is inspiration for continuous initiative to growth from within to full and prudent utilisation of all abilities of a person, that is, in other words, to self-realisation. Education of a free person lies in his appreciation of his role, relationship and responsibility to the physical and social environment in which he is cast, and at the same time experiencing of the deeper awareness within him that while he is in the world he is not of it. He may find himself caged in a body, impelled by the baffling powers of the mind and circumstanced by time and space; but nevertheless; he is still free, if he chooses to be so to explore his spiritual essence. The teacher is bound by a curriculum and he must teach subjects which he is called upon to teach; but most powerful influence of his personality lies in 'the hidden curriculum' of his personality and silent message which is excluded by his way of thinking, discipline of mind and refinement of tastes. A man is what he loves and cares for.

A teacher must no doubt teach certain subjects. The purpose is not merely to impart knowledge of the subject and help to train the mind of the pupil in the discipline of thinking characteristic of the subject and to apply what he learns to what he needs. He is expected to relate what he teachers, through processes of formal and non-formal instruction, to the wider objectives of education, viz. cultivation of spirit of independent enquiry and sensitiveness to moral obligations and good tastes. Moral values have bearing on the context of social life and human relationship.

Social history is a continuing experiment, often silent and unconscious; but sometime deliberate and violent, for adjustment between individual and social growth. It happens sometimes that a society striving for security and survival in the internationally competitive communities and maximisation of economic efficiency tends to exercise strangle-hold on the individual and dwarf his personality.

Strange phenomena sometime overtake the people - senseless struggle for power leading to wars, oppression of the weak, threats unleashed by piling of nuclear and other weapons of destruction; development of industries in some countries with consequent economic enslavement of the less developed countries; defilement of environment and massacre of forests, these and other fears exercise the minds of the thinking people. The teacher must ever be alert and watch out what may affect the future of humanity. The future is before him in the classroom; in the youth under his tutelage. His main concerns would obviously be to strive to cultivate interests and skills necessary for responsible evaluation of the social and human context and abilities to formulate judgements and provide correctives necessary to remove prevailing imbalances with a view to enabling full freedom for growth both for the individual and the society and to preserve the society from the threatening ills.

The teacher should therefore learn to appreciate and evaluate the context of the contemporary social life and the factors that condition it. He should also learn to invite and encourage pupils to contemplate in a detached, dispassionate and objective manner on the social trends of his times and to have visions of life as ideally lives as well as of effective and peaceful methods of social change. In order to be able to perform this function satisfactorily, the teacher has to be well-informed of the currents and cross-currents, historical and ideological, which influence life. The teacher should cultivate silent, sober, and serene detachment to sense what ails the individual and the society and to read the writing on the wall and to appreciate where humanity is drifting to.

In most of the schools the teacher is in contact with his pupils during the school or college working hours— five or six hours. After these school hours the educational process does not come to a stop nor does the pupil hybernate. In fact, more-compelling and alluring and indeed more effective processes of education or miseducation keep operating in the world outside the school. The environment, natural and at home and outside, keeps shaping the mind of the young. There was never any time a choice between 'education' and 'no-education', for to live itself is education. It was said at one time that to live in the Athens of Pericles was the best of education. The choice always is between 'bad' education and 'good' education.

At no time in the history of mankind, the forces of communication technology—the film, radio, TV, the newspaper—keep influencing the mind all the time. The hypnotic orator of deception has been perfected by politicians. The conduct of many of our leaders and functioning of social and political institutions do not go unnoticed by the youth. Blatant corruption and its callous tolerance; low means and shortcuts to power and wealth; the manner in which civic and political institutions are run; the way the government offices and officers function; the devices by which elections are fought and positions of power gained; these and several other factor exercise influence on the youthful minds and they are some times reflected and rehearsed in the elections to the college/ university unions and the perpetual war against the university authorities.

Increasing instances of brutal violence, tardy justice, all too concerned for natural justice to the culprit and totally unconcerned for any justice to the wronged, robbed and slaughtered, seem to make the youth feel that laws an made to defeat justice. These and other factors build in the minds of the youth a moral attitude and encourage permissiveness. The youth is intelligent enough to realise what deliberate misuse of some otherwise unexceptional concepts—democracy, socialism, liberty of expression, rights of minorities and weaker sections of society, and other similar concepts is made for the benefit of a few and the worst crimes are committed in the name of social and political catchwords. Dostoevsky repeatedly warned against playing irresponsibly with abstract ideas, e.g. democracy, socialism, liberty, equality and so on—because 'ideas have consequences'. There is enough experience of how these good concepts are used and what strage ends they are made to serve. Whitehead pointed out that great ideas enter reality in strange disguises and disgusting alliances. Roszak draws attention to the vexing paradoxes of modern industrial and technological age, viz. that intensified progress seems to be bound up which intensified unfreedom and thanks to communication technology, irrationality acquires character of rationality.

It is in this background that the teacher is expected to keep himself vigilant and provide models of sobriety and cool observation and thinking. Never before the task of the teacher was more challenging nor was he expected to wage of longer struggle with himself to keep his poise, clarity of vision and sobriety of judgement. This self-discipline on the part of the teacher cannot be taken for granted; he had to be given opportunities for learning to exercise self-discipline to keep him cool in the bewildering phenomenon of life. Neitzche compared an educated person to a tight rope walker; all the drum beating and noises, and the jostling of the crowds around him would not disturb his balance. This virtue cannot be imparted through formal classroom instruction. If the teacher has it, the pupil will hopefully have it.

Tradition is said to bring to teachers respect of the pupil and the society alike; but this tradition has received shocks in recent times and the teachers cannot take respect for granted. He has to earn in the hard way and to merit it. His scholarship and sincerity of purpose would no doubt command respect; but the teacher is not invariably expected to be bright. Only a few teachers are bright. His real influence lies in what he is and what he makes of himself.

The teacher's influence is not confined to what he does during his teaching hours in the classroom; in reality he teaches all the time. He is constantly watched by hundred of pairs of eyes; the way he walks and talks, studies and prepares his lessons; conducts himself inside and outside the classroom; the company he keeps; his habits of living, thinking and studying the way he treats his family and employees and all that he does is watched. The teacher lives in a glass house; he has hardly any private life. He is the observed of all observers and what he does tends unconsciously to be mimicked by the students.

The teachers thus provide models—good or bad—of behaviour for the pupils. Mimickry is the silent tribute the pupil pays to the teacher. This imposes on a teacher responsibility which is in some way unique. Educational literature sometimes refers to 'man-making', as one major concern of teacher education. Whatever may be understood by the term 'man-making', the more important function of teacher education should be to provide environment, inspiration, opportunities and all these are necessary to help the teacher to 'make himself', in other words, to cultivate his personality and to realise the best he is capable of. He has to learn to mould his life-style, his habit of walking, talking, laughing, working, thinking and conducting himself in public or private life.

The most valuable and enduring influence of a teacher a lies in the silent power of example. In ancient India the pupil lived with the teacher in sylvan hermitage in an atmosphere of solitude and silence. The pupil watched his teacher and imbibed the inward methods of the functioning of the teacher's mind, the secrets of his efficiency, the sources of his insprings of happiness, and the spirit of his life and world.

A disciplined teacher, correct and orderly in his habits, sensitive to the needs of those less fortunate in life, gracious and magnanimous; in his dealings with those around him, unruffled by the storms that blow around him, unwilling to stoop to whatever is mean and low however gainful it may be, always cheerful and pleasant without being vulgar and boisterous, will influence much better than through eloquent lectures. Whether in performance in any situation, the power of the teacher's will and his resolute defiance of difficulties constitute education which no formal teaching can provide.

The teacher must learn to acquire faith in himself. It is not less important that he should have faith in his student and in his capacity to develop all his powers and to build up his individual personality. One malady that characterises the educational system at present is the practice of passing judgements on the students and declaring them good or bad, worthy or unworthy, successful or unsuccessful. This is followed up by hero-worship and special rewards for those who are declared successful and even unconscious disincentive for those declared failures. Judgements of this kind must stop.

The teachers should appreciate that traditionally accepted educational methods inhibit full growth of man and create artificial values for evaluation of human spirit. It may even be said that the present system of evaluation in the system of education defeats full growth of man and develoment of several valuable human qualities. It is no wonder that some men who fortunately missed education achieved great heights in various levels.

The world was not lacking in great and good men before the system of schooling came into being. It is no wonder that thinkers like Iwan llich suggest de-schooling of society. The achievements of the school are not only limited but tend to create wrong human values. The teacher, therefore, must learn to adopt a wider view of education and desist from the practice of passing judgement on the student on the basis of schools and examination records. He would err on the right side if he assumes that there can be wrong syllabus, wrong curriculum, wrong textbooks, everything wrong, but not wrong pupil. Teacher's faith in the pupil and his endeavour to help him to discover himself is real education. It is the teacher's responsibility to understand his pupil independently of the customary categorisation fashionable in the system of education.

There is at present a growing concern for helping the student to acquire social skills and relevant knowledge which would enable the pupil to live in a society which is getting more and more complex and to participate in the social, economic and political process that affects its destiny.

Participation in social and national life and cultivation of human attitudes and sense of social justice and respect for other persons' point of view are no doubt essential parts of proper education. It is equally important for the teacher to appreciate that a man has also to live with himself and he cannot run away from himself. The most important things happen to man in solitude. The most important decision are taken, new discoveries are made, and novelties perceived in the loneliness of the mind.

The teacher must have a philosophy of his own which should be reflected in his behaviour; but he would be misunderstood if he confined himself to airy abstractions. He must also be a down-to-earth realist and his sense of realism should be reflected in his relationship with the subjects he teaches. It would be sad if the pupil got the impression that the teacher teaches certain subjects only because he is hired and paid for it and that he is no better than any other mercenary. Such a teacher may enable the student to pass an examination, but he will command little respect. What affects the students' mind and attitude is the devotion of the teacher to his subjects and his genuine involvement in its development. His seriousness in his studies and in struggling with the many problem arising out of it, his joy in discovery of novelty in the course of his studies become infectious for his pupils.

The teacher who merely repeats a laboratory experiment mechanically and purposelessly as a matter of prescribed drill, the teacher who teaches geography and astronomy without looking out or gazing at the skies at night, the teacher who teaches history out of books and is uninterested in local history and ancient monuments, will not kindle fire in the minds of the pupils. He should not be surprised if he gets a cold reception from his class. The enthusiasm and commitment of the teacher to his subject and his ability to inspire and arouse interest in the minds of the students determines the quality of the teacher.

The teacher must also be aware of the best known methods of teaching the subjects he teaches and he should learn those methods by practising them. But he should be a master of methods and not a blind follower of the fashionable ones. Methods of teaching are experiments the results of which need constant watching. Methods need to be refined continually in the light of the results achieved. Methods are personal and depend largely on the teacher's concept of what he aims to do and his imaginative approach to putting his ideas across to the pupil in order to inspire him to learn. The teachers must be constantly aware of the methods used by other teachers and also testing the methods of teaching he adopts.

8

Teacher Training Programmes

Teacher education is an integral component of the educational system. It is intimately connected with society and is conditioned by the ethos, culture and character of a nation. The constitutional goals, the directive principles of the state policy, the socio-economic problems and the growth of knowledge, the emerging expectations and the changes operating in education, etc. call for an appropriate response from a futuristic education system and provide the perspective within which teacher education programmes need to be viewed.

When India attained freedom, the then existing educational system was accepted as such because it was thought that an abrupt departure from the same would be disturbing and destabilising. Thus a predisposition to retain the system acquired preponderance and all that was envisaged by way of changes was its rearrangement. Consequently, education including teacher education largely remained isolated from the needs and aspirations of the people. During the last five decades certain efforts have been made to indigenize the system. The gaps, however, are still wide and visible. The imperatives for building the bridges may be as follows:

— to build a national system of teacher education based on India's cultural ethos, its unity and diversity synchronising with change and continuity.

— to facilitate the realization of the constitutional goals and emergence of the new social order.

— to prepare professionally competent teachers to perform their roles effectively as per needs of the society.

— to upgrade the standard of teacher education, enhance the professional and social status of teachers and develop amongst them a sense of commitment.

These are but a few of the major concerns which call for an immediate action. A comprehensive, dynamic and responsive system of teacher education needs to be continually evolved keeping the overall scenario in view.

The need for improved levels of educational participation for overall progress is well recognised. The key role of educational institutions in realising it is reflected in a variety of initiatives taken to transform the nature and function of education — both formal as well as non-formal. Universal accessibility to quality education is considered essential for development. This has necessitated improvement in the system of teacher education so as to prepare quality teachers.

Various Commissions and Committees appointed by the Central and the State Governments in recent decades have invariably emphasised the need for quality teacher education suited to the needs of the educational system. The Secondary Education Commission observed that a major factor responsible for the educational reconstruction at the secondary stage is teachers' professional training. The Education Commission stressed that 'in a world based on science and technology it is education that determines the level of prosperity, welfare and security of the people' and that 'a sound programme of professional education of teachers is essential for the qualitative improvement of education.'

India has a large system of education. There are nearly 5.98 lakh Primary Schools, 1.76 lakh Elementary Schools and 98 thousand High / Higher Secondary Schools in the country, about 1300 teacher education institutions for elementary teachers and nearly 700 colleges of education / university departments preparing teachers for secondary and higher secondary schools. Out of about 4.52 million teachers in the country nearly 3 million are teaching at the primary/ elementary level.

A sizeable number of them are untrained or under-trained. In certain regions, like the North-East, there are even under-qualified teachers. As far as in-service education is concerned the situation is not very encouraging. It is estimated that on an average 40% of the teachers are provided in-service teacher education once over a period of five years. Regarding non-formal education, though a number of models are in vogue in various states in the country, much more needs to be done to prepare teachers and other functionaries for the system.

The Programme of Action (POA) has emphasised teacher education as a continuous process, its pre-service and in-service components being inseparable. The POA, among others, has pointed out the following in respect of teacher education :

a) Professional commitment and overall competencies of teachers leave much to be desired ;

b) The quality of pre-service education has not only not improved with recent developments in pedagogical science, but has actually shown signs of deterioration;

c) Teacher education programmes consist mainly of pre-service teacher training, with practically no systematic programmes of inservice training, facilities for which are lacking.

d) There has been an increase in sub-standard institutions of teacher education and there are numerous reports of gross malpractices; and

e) The support system provided by the State Councils of Educational Research and Training (SCERTs) and the University Departments of Education has been insufficient and there is no support system below the state level.

In pursuance of the NPE 1986 a major step was taken by the Central Government to enhance the professional capacity of a large number of teacher education institutions. Nearly 430 District Institutes of Education and Training (DIETs) have already been established by 1997-98. The DIETs are charged with the responsibility of organising pre-service and in-service programmes in addition to being the nodal resource centres for elementary education at district level. Likewise, Colleges of Teacher Education (CTEs) and Institutions of Advanced Study in Education (IASEs) have been given the responsibility of introducing innovations in teacher education programmes at the secondary and higher secondary stages and in vocational education.

The National Council for Teacher Education (NCTE) as a non-statutory body (1973-1993) took several steps as regards quality improvement in teacher education. Its major contribution was to prepare Teacher Education Curriculum Framework in 1978. Consequently, teacher education curricula witnessed changes in teacher preparation programmes in various universities and boards in the country. A similar effort was made in 1988.

During the last decade, new thrusts have been posed due to rapid changes in the educational, political, social and economic contexts at the national and international levels. Curriculum reconstruction has also become imperative in the light of some perceptible gaps in teacher education. Teacher education by and large, is conventional in its nature and purpose. The integration of theory and practice and consequent curricular response to the requirements of the school system still remains inadequate. Teachers are prepared in competencies and skills which do not necessarily equip them for becoming professionally effective. Their familiarity with latest educational developments remains insufficient.

Organised and stipulatory learning experiences whenever available, rarely contribute to enhancing teachers' capacities for self-directed life long learning. The system still prepares teachers who do not necessarily become professionally competent and committed at the completion of initial teacher preparation programmes. A large number of teacher training institutions do not practice what they preach. Several of the skills acquired and methodologies learnt are seldom practiced in actual school system. This highlights the need to bring realism and dynamism in the curriculum.

The Constitution of India solemnly resolves "to constitute India into a sovereign, socialist, secular and democratic republic and secure to all its citizens: justice-social, economic and political; liberty of thought, expression, faith, belief and worship; equality of status and of opportunity; and to promote among them all fraternity assuring the dignity of the individual and the integrity of the nation." These are the main goals which the nation expects to be realised through education. Teacher preparation must not lose sight of this basic thrust so as to empower teachers to inculcate the same among the students.

In order to reinforce faith in democratic socialism, secularism, justice, liberty, freedom etc. the role of education needs to be understood in its true perspective. Democracy is a process of building consensus among the citizens on matters of common concern. It expects high morality from them, protects the interest and preserves their uniqueness, dignity and individuality. Quality of democracy depends on its citizens willing to discharge their responsibilities towards the self, the family, the community, the nation and humanity at large. Democracy is a way of life and its values need to be imbibed through education and practised in the day-to-day life. Democratic socialism attempts to achieve a synthesis between individual freedom and social compulsion and combines liberty with responsibility and authority with accountability. The Indian situation demands citizens capable of making conscious and purposive efforts directed towards social cohesion and living together harmoniously.

Indian Society is plural and heterogeneous with an underlying current of unity. The imposition of a homogeneous and uniform curriculum of teacher education may prove counter productive under this situation. Except for identifying certain basics and essentials, regional autonomy must be exercised for developing region/culture specific curriculum of teacher education. Indian reality demands that plurality should be used for strengthening national solidarity and social cohesion.

The Indian state is secular. The Indian society, however, is religious. To resolve this dichotomy between the state and polity, the principle of equal respect for all the religions has been accepted. This is the essence of Indian secularism. The teachers themselves have to internalise the imperatives of secularism in national context and interpret the same effectively to the learners. That alone would develop the right attitudes among all citizens irrespective of their own backgrounds. In India religion is also the source of value and morality. The teachers have to develop values and morality in a different context. Teacher education has to respond to this reality.

Justice, liberty, equality of status and of opportunity and promoting fraternity constitute another set of inter-related goals. Justice protects the rights of the weak and ensures impartiality. To ensure justice and fulfil the constitutional commitments in this regard, certain positive and legal provisions have been made by the state. Special measures such as reservation in educational institutions, financial support, scholarships, hostel facilities, etc. have been extended to the under-privileged groups like Scheduled Castes, Scheduled Tribes, Other Backward Classes etc. It implies change in attitudes and values through education, in which the role of teachers needs to be stressed.

Liberty of thought, expression, faith, belief and worship is another constitutional goal which education is expected to help realise. Indian Constitution ensures equality of status and opportunity to all its citizens. The objective is to minimise social and economic disparities, inequality of power and life chances by positive discrimination in favour of the weak. The education of teachers should equip them with the competencies needed to deal with discrimination, disparities and inequalities. Fraternity stands for acceptance of universal brotherhood, respect for human personality and feeling of oneness irrespective of linguistic, racial, cultural and religious diversities.

PROBLEMS IN TEACHER EDUCATION

It is universally acknowledged that education is an effective means for social reconstruction and to a great extent it offers solutions to the problems a society is faced with. These problems may be economic, social, cultural, political, moral, ecological and educational. Since the teachers play a major role in education of children, their own education becomes a matter of vital concern. Teacher education must, therefore, create necessary awareness among teachers about their new roles and responsibilities.

Education of teachers needs to strengthen and stress upon the main attributes of a profession, such as, the systematic theory, rigourous training over a specified duration, authority, community sanction, ethical code and culture, generating knowledge through research and specialisation. It is acknowledged that formal professional training on continuous basis is necessary for becoming a good teacher as it caters to the development of one's personality and sharpening of communication skills and commitment to a code of conduct.

Economic Problems

Poverty, unemployment, and low rate of growth and productivity are some of the major economic problems of the country which have led to the compulsions of the backward economy. These problems seek immediate solution and demand a realistic co-ordination between economic planning and manpower planning.

Education can help find solutions if it is properly coordinated with manpower needs. Introduction of work education and vocationalisation of education in secondary schools will have to be given a modern and meaningful direction. The attitude towards the work culture needs a transformation. The Indian society needs education with special emphasis on science and technology, vocational inputs and realistic work experiences.

Teacher education curriculum, therefore, has to promote such attitudes as are necessary for the emergence of a new economic order. Alongwith the vocational competencies and skills a new work culture will have to be created which necessarily involves the inculcation of dignity of work, the spirit of self-reliance and scientific temper among students. The courses of teacher education need to be enriched to enable teachers to understand the attributes of modernity and development.

Social Problems

Casteism, communalism and regionalism are some of the problems in the body politic of the society which misguide the youth. Increasing delinquency, violence, terrorism and fissiparous tendencies and use of inappropriate means to get one's ends served are threats to the national integration and social cohesion. Democracy, violence and terrorism cannot coexist. Education has to develop a peace loving personality and the programme of teacher education has to contribute in this regard.

The explosion of population with all its allied disturbing trends is not only neutralising the economic gains but also creating many problems for the country. Indian society still suffers from evils like child labour, child marriage, untouchability, discriminatory treatment to women, violation of human rights, etc. and most of the people are unaware of their legal rights.

Modern model of development which puts man against nature by making it an object of exploitation has disturbed the harmony and equilibrium between the two. Its consequences are visible in serious environmental degradation, pollution and ecological imbalances.

Strengthening national and social cohesion in a diverse and plural society, accelerating the process of economic growth, improving the life of the downtrodden and the people living below the poverty line, removing the widely prevalent ignorance, superstition and prejudices from the masses, inculcating scientific temper and developing a critical awareness about the social realities of Indian life are some of the issues which call for immediate attention. Teachers and the teacher educators have a special role to play in such efforts.

Problems of Cultural Reconstruction

Education is the process of transmission of dynamic and responsive components of cultural heritage and its continuous enrichment. There is a need to reinterpret the Indian culture in its distinct identity and composite strength. Its capacity to absorb the sublime from the other cultures needs to be highlighted. The teachers will have to play their role in cultural transmission and reconstruction.

Crises of Values and Morality

There has been a persistent erosion of values in the society. In the present day context certain values need to be redefined and reinstalled. There are situations when the values imparted and inculcated in schools are not generally practised in society. Value education demands a planned and purposive approach. It is through education and as of necessity through teacher education programmes that the task of inculcating values can be substantially accomplished.

Whereas values are emotive, the other related significant dimension is that of moral education which is essentially conative in character. Morals are situation-specific and demand immediate decision and action and yet there are morals which are considered to be eternal and universal. Through committed teachers, the art of ensuring moral development in a secular, multi-religious and multi-ethnic society needs to be cultivated.

Problems within Education System

The nation has yet to fulfil the constitutional commitment to provide free and compulsory education to all children till they attain 14 years of age. India is also a party to the global commitment for achieving the goal of Education for All by the year 2000. The education system however, has to respond to several major issues and problems which have hindered the progress in this regard. Maintenance of educational standards against the pressure of increasing enrolment, relevance and quality of school education, efficacy of school functioning under the decentralized role of political power through the enactment of Panchayati Raj Act are some of the pertinent issues.

In addition, specific requirements and need of social and economical groups of the society and of the minority communities, vocationalization of education, scientific and technological literacy, alienation of youth, rush for urbanisation, perceived urban orientation of educational system and its inflexibility to respond to rural, tribal and regional requirements are some of the dominant issues. These would determine the nature and shape of teacher education programmes and the efficacy and functioning of teachers in their new and emerging multifaceted roles.

Isolation of Teacher Education

Teacher education institutions which were considered 'islands of isolation' have gradually developed linkages with schools, peer institutions, universities and other institutions of higher learning as also the community. However, much remains to be done in this direction. The curriculum of the school, its actual transactional modalities, examination system, management processes and its ethos need to be the main thrust areas of teacher education programmes. To achieve these ends, teacher educators need to be made conversant with various aspects of school experiences. It is observed in day-to-day functioning that teacher educators often tend to lose contact with content areas relevant to their own disciplines resulting into gaps in communication and latest information. It is, therefore, a felt need in the present-day context that teacher education institutions keep in continuous touch with institutions of higher learning and peer institutions for effective transmission of knowledge and its upgradation.

The breaking of isolation from the community is essential for enabling teachers and teacher educators to reconstruct pedagogical and educational principles and practices in the light of experiences gained from mutually beneficial community interactions. Teacher as a professional and intellectual cannot remain indifferent to the events that are taking place in society. The academic and social issues are inter-related and inter-dependent. In contemporary context, the role of the teacher is no longer confined to teaching alone. The teachers are expected to play an active role in the developmental activities responding to progress of the community.

Expanding Scope of Teacher Education

Education of teachers is not an end in itself. Its target is the school. Any change in the nature, purpose, quality and character of the school demands a concomitant change in teacher education, specially in its curriculum. The implementation of the 10 + 2 scheme at the school level has transformed the complexion of education to a considerable extent from the pre-primary to the + 2 stage. There has been an increase not only in the quantum of knowledge, but also in its nature and purpose. In addition, new transactional techniques and strategies have also been evolved. Certain new subjects have replaced the old ones whereas some others have changed their context, content, orientation, theme and philosophy. These changes at the school level, out of necessity, demand a new pedagogy and evaluation techniques. But the changes at the level of teacher education have not adequately responded to the emerging realities at the school level. All that the teachers are expected to do in their work places need to be reflected in the teacher education activities and programmes.

The teaching community has to face the challenges thrown by science and technology. There has been an explosion not only of scientific and technological knowledge but also in the means and techniques of acquiring knowledge. The scientific researches and developments related to theories of heredity, learning, mental health, neurology, attention, motivation etc. can no longer be treated alien to teacher education programmes.

Evolving a Culture-Specific Pedagogy

Every region and state has its typical cultural identity, and there is a need to utilise the same as a basis for developing meaningful, relevant pedagogies. Since there is no one universal way in which the children learn, there is a strong need for looking into the cultural context in which a child is placed. A child in a tribal society may process information in an altogether different manner as compared to the one from the urban area and high socio-economic stratum. Pedagogy, therefore, should be culture-specific. Cultural practices such as story-telling, dramatics, puppetry, folk-play, community living, etc. should become a strong basis of pedagogy instead of using one uniform, mechanistic way of student learning. Cultural specificity should get embedded in the pedagogical practices which should be evolved for tribal, rural, urban communities and other ethnic groups.

Institutional Functions

In the light of context and concerns teacher education institutions will acquire a wider spectrum of functions and greater responsibilities. Resolution of specific functions from the spectrum will have to be made depending upon the institutional capabilities. It is visualised that the following institutional functions will have to be undertaken by different institutions according to availability of resources :-

— develop capability to provide for both pre-service and in-service education.

— provide training and orientation programmes to the functionaries of alternative educational strategies aimed at achieving universal elementary education and eradication of illiteracy.

— organise programmes for heads of schools and school complexes and supervisory staff.

— offer courses for community leaders, voluntary agencies and parents.

— provide academic support to schools and other agencies engaged in education of children and adults.

— undertake research and experiments with innovative educational ideas.

— act as a resource centre for education for a specific area.

— offer counselling and guidance services.

— organise need-based programmes for educational administrators, planners, curriculum designers, evaluators etc.

— impart training for other areas of education, like physical education and special education.

— act as a link between the school and the university system.

PERFORMANCE IN TEACHER EDUCATION

A major concern in school education is the quality and relevance of education being imparted to young learners. Every learner is supposed to acquire mastery level learning in identified competency areas. NCTE has analysed the existing curriculum of teacher education from the point of view of competency areas. It has emerged that to enhance the quality of school education equal emphasis needs to be given to competencies, commitment and willingness to perform.

A curriculum framework based upon competencies, commitments and performance has been developed. Competency areas namely, contextual competencies, conceptual, content, transactional, related to other educational activities, developing teaching learning material, evaluation, management, working with parents and working with community and other agencies, have been identified as critical to teacher preparation at elementary stage.

Acquisition of competencies alone will not be sufficient until and unless the teacher is fully committed. Teacher commitment areas identified include commitment to the learner, commitment to the society, commitment to the profession, commitment to attaining excellence for professional actions and commitment to basic values.

Alongwith competency and commitment areas, performance areas have also been identified. These include classroom performance, school level performance, performance in the out-of school educational activities, parents related performance and community related performance. Teacher education institutions could identify details in each of the three major categories. For each competency, commitment and performance area, the existing curriculum needs to be analyzed. Whenever certain unit of curriculum is taken up for transaction, its relationship to commitment and performance has to be examined. Such an approach would provide an opportunity to the training institutions to prepare teachers who are not only competent but also committed and both these aspects are reflected in their performance leading to higher learning attainments by all children.

Pre-service Teacher Education

Teacher education by its very nature is interdisciplinary. The major areas of inter-disciplinarity implicit in teacher education programmes include philosophy, psychology, sociology, anthropology, economics, history and culture. Recent researches in medical and life sciences are opening new avenues of knowledge which are relevant to education. Besides, teacher education has an essential and inalienable component of practical work including student teaching, internship, field work, working with the community, work education, etc. The country needs teachers with different orientation and specialisations to manage educational programmes. In addition, the teachers are also needed for physical education, music, art, painting, dance, work education and vocational subjects and for the non-formal stream, distance education, adult education, and open learning system. The scope of teacher education curriculum, therefore, gets enlarged.

The curriculum for teacher preparation, in future has to emcompass the broader canvas which is consistently emerging before the teachers and shall continue to change at a much faster pace in times ahead. Teachers shall have to take a global view of the new trends, strategies and practices, and focus on indigenous heritage and thoughts which could fit in the local and national situations. Transplantation of alien educational ideas and practices has not been found rewarding in developing countries. Consequently, the emerging structures and designs of the curriculum shall lay greater emphasis on the ideas, practices and experiences that have emerged in India through the contributions of thinkers like Mahatma Gandhi, Vivekanand, Rabindra Nath Tagore, Zakir Hussain, Sri Aurobindo, Giju Bhai and many others.

The teacher education programmes shall focus on competencies and commitment in much greater magnitude in future. Such a transformation in teacher preparation strategies would emerge only after due familiarity and adequate appreciation of indigenous thoughts developed over decades in India. Gradually an indigenous approach and strategy would emanate and replace the alien practices that have remained in vogue in teacher education over the decades.

The profile of a teacher which emanates from the contexts and concerns necessarily implies additional roles besides the conventional ones. The following capabilities and competencies need to be highlighted:

— inculcating the intrinsic and extrinsic values of professional competency, professional commitment and professional ethics
— creating and reconstructing knowledge
— selecting, organising and using learning resources
— effectively transacting curriculum, selecting and organising educational activities and programmes for learners with special needs
— using media and appropriate instructional technologies
— communicating effectively and responding to the challenges of continuity and change
— counselling students for personality development, adjustment and learning attainment
— conducting research, especially action research and initiating innovative practices
— organising student-activities
— inculcating a sense of value judgement, value commitment and value transmission
— understanding the import of inter-relationship between culture and education and 'culture and personality'
— fostering interest in life-long learning
— understanding the aspirations and expectations of the community and establishing mutually supportive linkages between school and community

— acting as a change agent for modernisation and development

The educational programmes for prospective teachers, therefore, need to be so designed as to develop in them the requisite potential and capabilities.

General Objectives

The general objectives of teacher education derived from the contexts, concerns and issues of education, teacher education and the perceived profile of the teacher, could include the following:

— to promote capabilities for inculcating national values and goals as enshrined in the Constitution of India.

— to enable teachers to act as agents of modernisation and social change.

— to sensitize teachers towards the promotion of social cohesion, international understanding and protection of human rights and rights of the child.

— to transform student-teachers into competent and committed professionals willing to perform the identified tasks.

— to develop competencies and skills needed for becoming an effective teacher.

— to sensitize teachers and teacher educators about emerging issues, such as environment, ecology, population, gender equality, legal literacy, etc..

— to empower teachers to cultivate rational thinking and scientific temper among students.

— to develop critical awareness about the social realities.

— to develop managerial and organisational skills.

Characteristics of Curriculum Framework

An overview of the context and concerns as discussed earlier, teacher's profile and general and specific objectives would define the boundaries of a curriculum framework. The perceived characteristics of the envisaged curriculum framework would include the following:

— reflects the Indian heritage, acts as an instrument in the realisation of national goals and fulfills aspirations of people.
— responds to the latest developments in the field of education.
— establishes integration of theory and practice of education.
— provides multiple educational experiences to teachers.
— enables teachers to experiment with new ideas.
— ensures inseparability of pre-service and in-service education of teachers.
— sets achievable goals for various stages of teacher education.
— provides for use of communication technology.

In-service Teacher Training

In-service teacher education within the overall framework of teacher development, has a crucial role to play. It is no cliché but a reality that those who teach should never cease to learn. The National Policy on Education, 1986 stipulates that teacher education is a continuous process and its pre-service and in-service components are inseparable. The initiatives taken in setting up District Institutes of Education and Training (DIETs), Colleges of Teacher Education (CTEs), and Institutions of Advanced Study in Education (IASEs) are some of the major developments in this regard.

Professional development of teachers begins with pre-service and gets renewed through in-service programmes. It, however, does not mean that there is a simple linearity between the two. There are elements of 'change' and 'continuity' in teacher education system which necessitate renewal and upgradation of skills and competencies. The in-service programmes are also organised to sustain the 'survival competencies' which the teachers acquired years ago, during pre-service education.

In the professional updating of teachers, changes in the societal goals, educational structure, curriculum framework, transactional strategies, evaluation techniques and management processes play a significant role. New advances emerging on the educational horizon have to be addressed to and teachers made aware of the same as well.

Teacher development is a complex process. Teachers update themselves by putting in various efforts of self-learning, peer learning and interactions with the community. Other alternatives to professional development are participation in recurrent programmes, extension activities and continuing education programmes.

In-service teacher education programmes are essential in view of obsolescence as well as explosion of knowledge and are necessitated on account of changes in educational and social realities. Whenever teachers are required to execute new and different roles or get promoted to a position that requires new set of competencies, participation in appropriately designed in-service programmes is called for.

Advances in the fields of curriculum, evaluation, audio-visual aids, telecommunication, etc. demand updating and orientation of teachers. Innovations both at macro and micro levels, would fail if teachers are not equipped and properly oriented to implement. In the Indian context, the developments, such as the 10+2+3 pattern, the making of science compulsory upto class X, new practices in evaluation like internal assessment, question banks, continuous and comprehensive evaluation, scaling and grading, introduction of new areas like environmental education, population education, computer education, AIDS education, gender sensitivity, etc. demand in-service training of teachers.

In-service training programmes are offered in various ways. Resource institutions at the national level offer orientation programmes of varying duration for different target groups. Besides this modality there are others like attachments, visits, national exchange programmes and international study visits; which form a significant component of in-service programmes. The diagram I indicates various components which contribute to teacher development. Pre-service and initial teacher education is reinforced by self-initiated learning, in-service teacher education programmes and recurrent and continuing education. Self-initiated learning involves study on one's own for professional development. Recurrent and continuing programmes are organised through seminars, workshops, orientation courses etc. as per the professional requirements.

In-service teacher education broadly perform the following functions:

— updates teachers in issues concerning content, methodology and evaluation,

— upgrades serving teachers in tasks with which they are currently occupied,

— initiates and orients teachers to new roles and technologies,

— provides opportunities for unqualified or underqualified on-the-job teachers to update and upgrade their knowledge.

While content, design and duration of each programme would be determined by one or more functions identified above, long range efficacy of any programme would also be judged by its impact on the following:

— personality of the trainees;

— motivation and commitment in matters relating to professional and self growth;

— awareness of social realities; and

— communication and evaluative skills;

In-service teacher education has to be organised for achieving the following broad objectives :

- to upgrade the qualifications of under-qualified and/or untrained on-the-job teachers.
- to upgrade the professional competence of serving teachers.
- to prepare teachers for new roles.
- to provide knowledge and skills relating to emerging curricular changes - content, process and evaluation.
- to make teachers aware of critical areas and issues, like, competency-based learning, multigrade, multi-level and multi-channel teaching, teaching students of disadvantaged groups, meeting educational needs of children with learning problems, developing inquiry skills, use of mass media in education, community participation and educational development of dyslexic children.
- to overcome gaps and deficiencies of pre-service education.

In-service programmes need to be built around 'transformational objectives', i.e. increasing motivational level, enriching self-concept, building climate of inquiry and making teachers reflective practitioners. The thrust of transformational objectives is to develop such qualities in teachers as would enable them to become receptive, perceptive, reflective, innovative and dynamic.

Strategies

Strategies adopted in in-service teacher education programmes would vary programme-wise and theme-wise. One has to judiciously select an appropriate training strategy or a mix of training strategies keeping in view the theme, programme duration, background of participants, availability of resource persons, support material and technologies of training at hand.

Training strategies would range from lecture-cum-discussion to project work, library work, group interaction, field visits. There may be many models of in-service training. Some of these are given below:

Face to face Institutional Model

In this model, the training institution offers in-service training programme on its premises using direct face to face training approach. It is most effective when the number of participants is around 30 to 40. Besides lecture-cum-discussion mode many other transactional strategies are also used namely project method, case method, library work, peer learning sessions, buzz sessions, and small group techniques. The merit of this approach is that there is a direct and sustained interaction between participants and resource persons. The limitation of this approach is that it cannot be used when the institution wants to train a very large number of participants within a short time.

Cascade Model

In this model number of persons to be trained is very large and training design is built on two or three tier systems. In the first level the key resource persons are given training. They train resource persons who in turn train teachers. The advantage of this model is that a large number of teachers can be trained within a short duration of time. However, it has its limitations. Knowledge and information passed on at the first tier of key resource persons and then at the second tier of resource persons get somewhat diluted resulting into transmission loss of training effectiveness.

Media Based Distance Education Model

With the advent of satellite technology and computers many training programmes are imparted using electronic media. Audio-conferencing and tele-conferencing are already being used. In these the electronic media play the key role and print material play a supportive role. The advantage of this model is that training objectives can be achieved within limited time period. The constraint of this approach is the limited availability of the technology itself, and its high initial investment.

Besides the above three models, some other important considerations contribute to effectiveness of an in-service training programme.

i) *Locale*: Training institutions at the national, state and district level organise training programmes generally at their respective institutions. These institution based trainings have their own strengths in terms of availability of resources. Their limitations are that they dislodge participants from their work place. This approach is often known as off-site approach. On the other hand using on-site approach many institutions organise training programmes at the school site itself. Thus participants are not dislodged from their work place. Extension programmes and on-site programmes take training to the doorsteps of schools/institutions.

ii) *Target Groups*: At present in-service programmes are organised largely for teachers. A few programmes are also organised for headmasters, principals and other supervisory staff. This net has to be widened and many more categories of personnel brought into the fold. In-service teacher education programmes ought to be offered to all teachers working at pre-primary, primary, elementary, secondary and senior secondary levels. These could cater to teachers working in formal schools, non-formal centres, open and distance teaching institutions and institutions of physical education, adult education, special education, etc.

Teacher educators, in general, have limited exposure to in-service education. There is a need to train teacher educators at all levels. In fact, an apex institution needs to be set up for training of teacher educators. Alternatively some selected institutions may develop special expertise in training of teacher educators. Such institutions would have to develop relevant support material and undertake critical research studies relevant to in-service programmes of teacher educators.

Besides teachers, supervisors and administrators, there are other categories like Zila Pramukh, Pradhan, Sarpanch etc. connected with Panchayat Raj System who have the responsibility to look after primary level education. Depending upon the resources available staff of the support system, including librarians, hostel wardens, etc. should also be exposed to various programmes to enhance their professional competence.

iii) *Transactional Strategies* : An effective in-service education and training programme would use various transactional strategies like case study method, brain storming sessions, panel discussions, seminars, symposia, small group techniques, project work, library work and lecture-cum-discussion sessions.

The organisers and the resource persons can make an in-service teacher education programme more effective and interesting if the age, experience and background of participants are appropriately used at the planning phase. Since in-service participants bring a lot of experience and way of looking at educational events, they can significantly contribute to the design and development of programmes.

iv) *Content :* Content of in-service programmes would depend upon objectives of each programme which could be grouped under the following major categories :

— school subjects.

— pedagogy and methodology.

— emerging issues.

— teacher's new role.

The focus of in-service programmes is on developing competencies and commitments. The overall aim of in-service programmes is to enable teachers to improve their classroom activities, out-of-the-classroom activities, school activities and community activities.

v) *Evaluation and follow-up :* Evaluation is a weak link in many in-service training programmes. In most of the cases in-service programmes are evaluated, if at all, on an *ad hoc* basis. Each in-service teacher education programme should have monitoring as an integral component so that effectiveness of a programme can be properly assessed and apraised. Programme evaluation should assess whether the required inputs were provided to the programme on time, the logistics properly looked after and coordinated, the reading materials provided to participants etc. Another aspect of programme evaluation should be to assess the gains of each participant. The other subtle aspect is the impact evaluation to assess the impact of the programme at the grassroot level and in the field situation.

Education and training programmes become more productive and effective when programme planning is participative and transactional strategies are interactive. The need of all in-service teacher education programmes must emerge from the grassroots. For example, under the centrally sponsored teacher education programme, District Institutes of Education and Training are expected to organise programmes for teachers in such a way that every elementary teacher gets a chance to participate in the programme of his or her choice at least once every five years. In this venture state level coordinating agency like SCERT can play a faciliative and co-ordinating role to ensure that need based in service programmes are launched.

In some states due to certain reasons and other considerations, untrained and under-qualified teachers get recruited. These untrained and underqualified teachers need training and content upgradation. The backlog of untrained and underqualified teachers has to be cleared at the earliest. Whenever teachers are promoted from elementary level to secondary level or from secondary level to senior secondary level, intensive in-service training programmes should be designed and offered to them. Whenever a teacher takes up new educational assignments, he/she would require task oriented in-service training.

There is a need to make a shift in organising programmes from training institutions to schools and school clusters. Concerted efforts may be made in this direction. Development of support material is very important for in-service education. Unless quality support materials are developed, face-to-face training alone may not be enough. Good quality support material in the form of print, video cassette and computer programmes have to be designed, developed and disseminated. Some in-service programmes be made credit oriented. On successful completion of specified programmes, participants may be considered for professional mobility.Participation in in-service programmes within a stipulated period should be made obligatory and appropriate incentives thought of.

9

Developing Effective Physical Education Teachers

Effective teachers have different styles and personalities, and are considered effective for varying reasons. In many communities, teachers are considered effective if many of their students attain some of the following: sound academic achievement; an enjoyment of learning; and skills to continue to learn, solve problems, and functionally operate in and contribute to their societies. Effective teachers give students appropriate attention when needs arise. Whatever other worthwhile results are achieved because of teachers' work, teacher effectiveness is usually expressed in terms of pupils' academic achievement, something that is more easily measured than some other valued outcomes of good education. The measurable gains in student progress are some of the strongest indicators of improvement in educational quality. Improving the learning environment will help raise student achievement. Teachers who are able to develop sound academic achievement with their pupils tend to share many of the following characteristics.

i) know their subject matter;

ii) use pedagogy appropriate for the content;

iii) use an appropriate language of instruction, and have mastery of that language;

iv) create and sustain an effective learning environment;

v) find out about and respond to the needs and interests of their students and communities;

vi) reflect on their teaching and children's responses and make changes to the learning environment as necessary;

vii) have a strong sense of ethics;

viii) are committed to teaching; and

ix) care about their students.

Ongoing, relevant staff development activities are necessary if a teaching force is to be effective. Adequate time and resources need to be set aside for teacher development, that staff members need to have a say in the content of activities, that skills learned should be practised over time with follow-up sessions implemented where necessary, and that staff members should be encouraged to share ideas and work together. Changed attitudes and behaviours and new skills and strategies are the result of most in-service programmes.

Effective teachers tend to have confidence in their ability to teach, care about teaching and their students, and cooperate with each other. These characteristics are reflected in the teachers' comfort in using learning materials and in trying new ideas, low teacher absenteeism and tardiness, and a high level of group involvement in planning teaching and in resolving whole-school issues. However, classrooms where teachers lack general subject mastery and confidence in their ability to teach, the development of positive teacher attitudes is often hindered.

Research has indicated the importance of the length of school study time on student learning and achievement. Children who spend more time studying in school tend to learn more. A distinction needs to be made between the established number of days and hours per day, the actual time the school is in operation, and how the available hours are used. In some settings, the policy on the school calendar and daily hours may need to be revised to have schools in session more. In others, the policy may be adequate, but school may, nevertheless, remain closed often, or the school day may be shortened, e.g., a leaky roof, teacher absenteeism, or overcrowded double sessions. Research from a variety of countries has shown that both the amount of time available for instruction as well as how this time is used by students and teachers is consistently related to how much children learn at school.

Initial Teacher Preparation Programmes

Teacher development means comprehensive growth and support. From the time teachers begin any initial preparation and/or teaching, provision needs to be made for ongoing development of knowledge of subject matter; concrete skills to teach, observe, assess, and reflect; incentives; and career growth. There also needs to be a linkage with other teachers and supervisors to help solve problems and to support each other through discussion, modelling, and coaching, and an involvement with other aspects of school and educational change. The isolation and lack of communication between all players need to be reduced.

Ministries of education and regional office staff have a responsibility to provide sufficient teaching and learning materials to support the curriculum, ensure adequate facilities, and provide ongoing support for the issues that teachers face. The appropriate length of initial preparation courses and their organisation is debatable. The reality is that there are a variety of ways to prepare and support teachers in a variety of environments. Just as there is no single type of effective teacher, but there are common elements associated with successful teachers, there is no single type of effective initial preparation course. But there are common elements that should be discussed and incorporated where appropriate in design and implementation.

Beginning teachers ideally need initial preparation in the subject matter they will teach, some basic strategies for how to teach that subject matter, verbal competency in an appropriate language of instruction, some instructional materials in an appropriate language for learning, knowledge of how to use these materials, some basic classroom skills concerning managing students and the learning environment, and basic skills in observation and reflection. While some information might be provided through lectures or seminars in a formal initial preparation programme, most of these practical skills are best learned through on-the-job practice with coaching.

Initial preparation of teachers varies greatly across countries. Success depends on how the courses are structured and what support accompanies them. Programmes that have shorter initial training tend to need more concentrated on-the-job followup; however, all programmes need ongoing job support. Where there is an issue with getting females trained in restricted social regions, mobile teacher training has proved helpful.

Well designed distance education programmes can provide training to teachers, especially to large numbers of teachers. The point is that a range of alternative initial programmes that might match local demands and conditions is available. The experiences of BRAC primary education programme, the rural community schools in Egypt, and the mobile teacher training programme in Pakistan offer ideas for addressing particular needs for getting more teachers quickly into schools in particular social contexts. All these projects demonstrated flexibility in selecting local people for training, taking them where they are at in experience, providing basic preparation, providing strong on-the-job support, and encouraging teachers to meet and work together to solve classroom problems all contribute to their success.

One serious omission, however, is often the accreditation. Accreditation ideally should accompany non-traditional training and continue over the following years. In order to provide equity between the status of teachers as well as develop uniform performance standards, accreditation needs to match the ongoing training undertaken by all teachers. A disservice is done to both teachers and the teaching profession if all teachers do not have the opportunity to gain equal professional qualifications, no matter what route is taken to attain them.

The more typical categories that initial teacher preparation programmes fall into, those at least that are considered formal and traditional "pre-service" programmes, tend to be:

i) Certificate or degree programmes housed in normal colleges, normal schools, and colleges of education established solely for the purpose of training teachers. These programmes usually specialise in training primary school teachers and emphasise pedagogical more than subject area preparation. These programmes tend to be two to four year programmes that lead to a certificate or diploma in teaching.

ii) Degree programmes housed at general, multipurpose universities. These programmes usually emphasise subject matter preparation more than pedagogical preparation. These are generally three or four-year programmes leading to a bachelor's degree, with the teaching preparation portion lasting one to two years.

iii) Master's degree and/or fifth year programmes. These programmes, open to candidates who have completed a bachelor's degree, lead to a master's degree or postgraduate diploma in education. The duration of these programmes ranges from one to two years beyond the bachelor's degree.

Traditional Teacher Preparation Programmes

Where governments wish to maintain and improve their traditional formal programmes for initial preparation of teachers, the following essential elements of coherent and successful teacher education programmes have been identified by researchers. In many ways the elements listed below are part of what constitutes essential components of good schools as well. While these tend to reflect the experience of resource rich countries, we believe the lessons are worth discussing for any formal teacher education programme:

i) Shared vision and conceptual framework for the programme
   a) Make expectations clear, develop faculty collegiality, and ensure programme renewal.
   c) Develop consensus about curriculum scope, sequence, integration, and articulation.
   d) Clarify what is valued in a teacher and what is expected of the prospective teacher.
   e) Acknowledge the realities of schools as places and the role that teachers play.
   f) Support an explicit coherent design for programmematic research and evaluation.
   g) Require goals that are clear and reasonable.

ii) Collaboration of faculty and students
   a) Since collaboration is related to ownership, shared beliefs, and motivation, it is a good strategy to involve students to some degree in the design and implementation of the programme and the work carried out in schools.
   b) Teacher educators who teach in field sites, work regularly in schools, or have had recent and relevant practical experience in schools can foster a sense of collegiality and collaboration among students and faculty.
   c) Having access to faculty, being assigned smaller classes to promote more personal interactions, and

working with faculty with site visits, etc., helps to show personal caring, an important part of any teacher-student relationship.

d) Many faculty resist the above suggestions because of their already heavy teaching loads and the need they have to protect their time to attend to their own research. Administrators need to address the work loads and reward systems in education departments if greater collaboration between faculty and students is to occur.

iii) A coherent conception of "learning to teach"

a) General pedagogical knowledge and beliefs include knowledge and learning skills about various strategies and arrangements for effective classroom management; instructional strategies for conducting lessons and creating learning environments; and knowledge about how learners learn and how that learning can be fostered by teaching.

b) Subject matter knowledge and beliefs include the facts, terms, and concepts of a discipline; the organising ideas and ways of thinking and arguing on the topic, and knowledge growth within the discipline to understand the best ways to teach the subject.

c) Professional studies are included in the programme, e.g., courses related to the profession of teaching such as educational psychology, history, sociology, and philosophy.

d) Supervised teaching practice is a key focus of the programme.

iv) A rigorous and academically challenging programme

a) Teacher education has suffered from a widespread perception that no special knowledge base is required for teaching, that anyone can teach as long as they understand the mechanics of chalkboard use. Lax admission standards have reinforced these misconceptions.

b) Teacher education programmes must have a strong emphasis on academic rigour and provide challenging intellectual experiences for student teachers.

v) A curriculum structure that is integrated, develop-ment-oriented, and balanced.

a) Curricula that are developmental start from observation and move to practice. They also move from technical to multidimensional approaches to teaching.

b) There is sufficient time and discussion of concepts learned on campus and in school experiences to be synthesised and integrated. Key concepts need to be revisited over time.

c) Teacher educators model good teaching practices rather than talk about them.

d) There is an emphasis on mastery and depth of subject matter.

vi) Presence of student cohort groups

a) Just as teachers need other teachers with whom to discuss issues, developing cohort groups helps reinforce students' commitments to teaching as a career as well as provide academic and personal support throughout the course.

b) Faculty tend to feel greater accountability to a cohort than to individual students who come together for certain classes only.

vii) Adequate curriculum materials, facilities, and resources

a) Efforts are made to make available uptodate materials and facilities including curriculum materials, instructional resources, information, and communication technologies.

   b) Adequate library resources are critical.

   c) When national education reforms concern curriculum materials, these need to be got to the teacher training facilities ahead of time so they can be quickly integrated into programmes.

viii) Research and theory-based programmes

   a) Successful programmes are based on sound research.

   b) Faculty need to be active in classroom and school research to be current with issues and changing demands on teachers.

   c) Action research is a useful tool in assisting student teachers look at the complexities of teaching and learning.

ix) Systematic and effective programme evaluation

   a) Evaluation results must lead to improved programmes and practice.

x) Reflective inquiry

   a) Reflection needs to go beyond the technical critiques and beyond personal meaning-making.

   b) Reflective inquiry entails thinking carefully and imaginatively about why things happen as they do in schools, and what alternatives might be created.

The move towards a general education degree for primary teachers has opened up opportunities for teacher trainees throughout the world who start off with the intention of becoming teachers but then wish to enter other professions. The effects in the United States have not been severe, due to a surplus of qualified teachers, but there have been rather severe consequences in many developing nations where both graduates of secondary and superior level teacher training programmes use the often free education in teacher training as a stepping stone to higher paying or more prestigious occupations. The move to general education programmes is in part an attempt to give teaching a status comparable to other professions. While there has been a trend to train primary school teachers as generalists, prepared to teach in all content areas, some educational systems such as those in Alberta, Canada and Chinese Taipei, require primary teachers to focus on a specific subject area.

Most national systems of education use more than one criterion for selection of candidates into teacher education programmes. Common processes include:

i) Successful completion of the minimum required period of schooling. Such a requirement is not always expected of primary teacher candidates in some developing countries where teacher education programmes may still be part of the upper secondary education system;

ii) Sitting for an entrance examination that might consist of scholastic achievement and general knowledge;

iii) Personal interviews to look for such characteristics as communication skills, language proficiency, commitment to teaching, prior preparation, and personality; and

iv) Submission of letters of reference for character and academic checks.

Student intake into teacher training institutions is usually determined by government bodies in collaboration with teacher education programmes.

While there is a national standard in many regions that candidates are usually expected to meet, the demand for teachers in many countries is so great that standards are not always maintained. Even in higher income countries, the difficulties of recruiting sufficient teachers in particular subject areas and in certain geographical locations is often severe. The importance of having command of the subject- matter knowledge, the skills to communicate effectively and create and sustain a learning environment, the language proficiency, and the commitment to teaching are identified frequently in the research literature as ideal criteria for the selection of candidates for teaching positions. In desperate circumstances, a willingness to learn and a commitment to teaching are essential; the subject-matter knowledge and appropriate skills can be developed through on-the-job support and in-service programmes.

For attracting appropriate candidates when there are teacher shortages, some suggestions that have monetary implications are:

i) Nationally widen access through the introduction of more flexible training courses, especially part-time training opportunities and shortened teaching certificate/degree courses.
ii) Recruit atypical candidates, e.g., mature-age, change-of-career candidates.
iii) Assist local administrative levels to decide what staff are needed in which areas.
iv) Provide bursary payments for trainees in shortage subjects.
v) Promote teaching through regular national advertising and publicity campaigns competing directly with the efforts of graduate recruiters in other sectors.
vi) Locate, in some local directorates and individual schools, the introduction of more flexible working arrangements, including part-time jobs, job sharing, and career breaks.
vii) Retrain teachers to help reduce the problems of subject mismatch and hidden shortages.

Effective In-service Programmes

In-service programmes are varied in nature and quality, and only some have undergone formal evaluations to determine effectiveness of different organisational deliveries and the effect on student achievement. Effective professional development programmes that are known to make a difference to the quality of teaching support teachers to develop their classroom practice. Programmes that provide further credentials are important for developing the professional status of teaching, establishing teaching standards, and assisting in career growth, etc. However these training programmes do not always provide adequate linkages and ongoing support with classroom practice, and therefore actual instructional practices are often not changed, and the quality of teaching and student learning is hindered.

Effective professional development programmes, particularly for those teachers with little or no teacher preparation, tend to have the following characteristics.

An initial determination of what are the needs, interests, and strengths of teachers and other staff is essential before professional development activities are designed. For example, do participants need an induction programme to support their initial teaching experience, and what training, if any, do they already have on which to build? Will the programme provide specific new knowledge and skills needed by the participants or is it for refining already acquired knowledge and skills? Does a programme for ongoing support need to be organised? Will this training improve student learning? How will this activity fit into the school's overall programme? This information is important to determine the goals, content, best delivery method, and evaluation of the activity, whether it be a specific in-service training programme or larger ongoing support programme. Teachers and other staff must have a say in what training and support they require if it is to be relevant to their needs.

Effective programmes are well planned, and tend to be formal in nature. Some of these programmes focus on improving the performance skills of individual staff, or on organisational or curricular issues that will affect the whole staff, and some programmes for small groups of staff. An overall strategic framework for the long-term effort is necessary. The overall planning needs to consider how various needs might be met: peer coaching; action research in the classroom or school; visits to other classrooms or schools; visits by outside specialists, officials, and consultants; meetings with parents and other community members; short meetings; whole day activities held at the school or another location; retreats for the entire staff; longer development workshops; whole semester release; use of teachers' centres; resources shared in school clusters; district level training; and long-term programmes in centralised institutions. The programmes also need to be structured to reduce anxiety and fear of change, and the activities proven to be clear improvements from existing practice.

Apart from close consultation about their needs, teachers, principals and other local participants along with administrative officials need to be involved in the next planning steps of the programme. Those programmes that involved participant teachers in the planning of such activities tended to have greater success in accomplishing their objectives than those without the assistance of the participants. The most effective and relevant in-service programmes are those that allow high levels of local participation in both the design and implementation. There is also sometimes a need to involve local parents and community members in some in-service programmes. Some teacher education programmes have been developed in local communities and later have been supported by central governments and international agencies.

In these programmes, teachers, principals, and teacher educators worked as a team in the school to educate the community about its schools, the curriculum, and to learn a great deal about the characteristics of the local children and families. Locally recruited teachers develop a special role as mediators between mainstream culture of the school and the local culture of the pupils.

The curriculum of the programme needs to provide a balance of pedagogy and subject matter as opposed to exclusive emphasis on one or the other. It should also include practical methods to teach subject matter, child development, and learning theories in ways that are relevant to the student context, ways to evaluate teaching and learning, multi-grade classroom management, and ways to develop parent-school-community relations through participatory learning strategies such as discussion, simulations, and teaching practices. Many teachers do not teach as effectively as they could because they do not understand students, how they learn, and classroom dynamics.

The pedagogical component of effective in-service programmes often contains four key elements:

i) methods for helping teachers acquire specific skills for teaching the existing curriculum;
ii) methods for teaching meaningful rather than just rote learning;
iii) methods for developing in pupils positive attitudes to lifelong learning; and
iv) methods for helping teachers engage in curriculum development.

There are five essential components should be in training programmes:

i) presentation of theory or description of skill or strategy,
ii) modelling or demonstration of skills or models of teaching,
iii) practice in simulated and classroom settings,
iv) structured and open-ended feedback about performance, and
v) implementation in the actual classroom.

However, the most critical component is that the in-service programmes include provision for ensuring implementation in the classroom of the acquired learning, and that ongoing support facilitates this.

While basic teaching and classroom management skills are important, especially for new teachers who may have little initial preparation for the job, it is also essential that teachers develop good evaluation and decision-making skills. Mastery of skills shaped by judgements about how student learning can best be achieved, and positive attitudes are important areas to develop. Peer coaching, self-evaluation, and reflective group discussion are some in-service techniques that might be adopted to enhance this critical thinking.

Teachers in rural areas face special problems that may need more emphasis in the in-service programmes—dealing with isolation, working within the local community values and expectations, multi-grade teaching techniques, administration of small schools and heavier workloads, rural familiarity and lack of privacy, difficult housing and sanitary conditions, safety and value concerns(particularly for female teachers), and resource acquisition issues.

Programmes that focus on continuous development to guide, monitor, and support necessary skills, knowledge, and new ideas tend to be more successful in bringing about change at the classroom level than those that seek quick fixes to fill up deficiencies or those that simply provide a qualification. In-service programmes typically focus on helping teachers implement new curricula in conjunction with state values and educational reforms. These are usually short, one-time programmes that are known not to be as effective as ongoing programmes that focus on guidance and support at the school level. This ongoing support is essential for effective transfer of skills and is easiest developed through the school-based model. The main support comes both from within the school environment (e.g., principal, other teachers) and personnel from the larger education system and community.

At the level of the principal, the quality of teachers' work and student learning tends to be enhanced when the principal:

i) sees that the resources are available to provide adequate support to teachers, sufficient learning materials, and well maintained learning facilities;

ii) pursues high instructional standards by clearly and frequently stating in concrete terms the school's mission, curricular goals, and expected teaching behaviour; clearly and frequently expresses high expectations of pupils and the school's focus on learning as its central purpose;

iii) coordinates and manages the learning process;

iv) communicates regularly and effectively with teachers, parents, and others in the community; and

v) maintains high visibility and accessibility to pupils, teachers, parents, and others in the community.

At the teacher level, support to help the application of new skills into the classroom includes:

i) coaching about classroom skills and management from mentors and peers;

ii) a continuing study group with other teachers with similar in-service experiences;

iii) coordination of the in-service with the regular supervision of teachers; and

iv) provision made for travelling consultants to visit teachers.

At the level of the larger education system, effective support happens when the system:

i) delegates authority and responsibility for improvement to the schools themselves;

ii) communicates expectations or exerts pressure for successful academic results;

iii) provides important services to schools such as advice and training about instructional practices and management, resources needed to achieve instructional goals, and protects the school from political turbulence; and

iv) monitors and evaluates schools' academic performance, recognises successes, and provides support to overcome weaknesses.

Motivation is likely to be enhanced for the in-service programme where increased salary or other benefits are ensured.

At the level of parents and community, support for the ongoing work of teachers may be in several forms:

1) seeing that pupils come to school healthy and prepared to learn;
ii) providing financial or material support for the school's operation;
iii) communicating frequently with school staff;
iv) assisting with instruction both at the school and in the home; and
v) assisting with school governance with meaningful authority.

The simplified list of key essential elements for professional development programmes would be that they:

i) focus on concrete and specific training for instructional and management practice;
ii) are appropriate to the current needs of the teacher;
iii) involve teacher and other staff in the planning and implementation of both short and long-term activities;
iv) include a balance of theory and practice;
v) include small-group workshops, peer observations and feedback, coaching, and demonstrations;

vi) ensure implementation in the classroom of the acquired learning

vii) provide continuous guidance and support;

viii) have the support and participation of the head teacher and other school leaders;

ix) enable participation through release time;

x) provide regular meetings for problem solving;

xi) fit within the context of the local community and school culture; and

xii) fit within the broad, long-term professional development and school improvement programme.

Feedback informing facilitators on the modes of presentation, involvement, relevance, adequacy of facilities, and instructors etc., is valuable. However, she states that an effective evaluation must also investigate whether attitudes and practices of participants have actually changed for the better, and whether these changes are manifested in classroom and school practices and processes.

In general terms, a good evaluation of an in-service teacher education programme should:

i) adopt an explicit standard to good in-service teacher education against which any particular in-service programme can be judged;

ii) value the effects of in-service programmes on teachers' needs for professional experiences;

iii) expect and appreciate inevitable differences among teachers and schools in efforts to change educational practices, and take a more longitudinal perspective on educational change that might occur as a result of in-service education;

iv) expand the venue for the evaluation beyond the in-service experience and into the school, classroom, or wherever change might be manifest; and

v) require the expenditure of more resources to conduct serious evaluations.

INCENTIVES

Iincentives included all the direct and indirect benefits offered to teachers as intrinsic motivators. More specifically, he states that direct monetary benefits are the package of teacher salary, allowance, and fringe benefits; indirect monetary benefits are all other financial resources offered to teachers. These might include:

i) professional support such as initial and ongoing training programmes, teacher guides, textbooks, instructional supervision; and

ii) personal support such as free or subsidised housing, food, or transportation.

Non-monetary benefits include professional status in the community, location of teaching position, recognition and approval by significant people associated with the teacher, etc. Different incentives work for different people at different stages of their careers. It is important to look at each community of teachers and to find out what would make a difference for those individuals to improve their teaching as well as their career satisfaction. These incentives should be appropriate to the needs of the teachers, and be compatible with both the resources available as well as the expectations from teachers' unions and other professional associations.

Many countries provide incentives such as salary differentials, transportation funds, extra vacation time for travelling long distances, bicycles, or housing to encourage teachers to work in isolated rural areas. Research has not been able to document a clear connection between these incentives and student achievement, but such a relationship would be extremely difficult to isolate. However, logic would tell us that having a teacher regularly present in a rural classroom is considerably more beneficial to student achievement than having no teacher at all.

Induction Programmes

Induction programmes that guide and support beginning teachers in their first year or two of teaching are essential to develop sound teaching practices as well as to retain teachers in the system. Some countries prefer school-based induction programmes, while others such as Israel, have induction programmes run by teacher colleges and the academic schools of education. Some key guidelines for running induction programmes are listed below:

i) Provide continuing assistance for beginning teachers to reduce the identified common problems that typically occur in the early stages of teaching.

ii) Support development of the knowledge and the skills needed by beginner teachers to be successful in their initial teaching position, and provide resources for instructional materials.

iii) Integrate beginning teachers into the social system of the school, the school district, and the community.

iv) Provide an opportunity for beginning teachers to analyse and reflect on their teaching.

v) Accompany reflection time with coaching from veteran support teachers.

vi) Increase the positive attitudes of beginning teachers toward teaching.

vii) Provide incentives and compensation to those participating in the programme, including the mentor teachers.

viii) Provide release time for observations of other teachers-coaching and planning is necessary for both mentors and beginning teachers.

ix) Waive formal appraisals and evaluations during the first year of teaching.

Training of Teacher Educators

The overall quality in education mainly depends on the quality of teachers and a sound programme of professional preparation of teachers is essential for imparting quality education. However, teacher educators' own education leaves much to be desired. Teaching is an art which can be inculcated through a series of well designed activities in respect of education and training of teachers and is equally valid for professional preparation of teacher educators. The teacher educators would not only be training pre-service and in-service trainees but would also be associating themselves with several other activities.

New strategies and techniques of material development, the changing approach to evaluation, intensive interactions with the community, creating an activity-based environment in the training institutions, acquiring skills for resource mobilisation and several other such competencies at mastery level would be essential for professionals to function as teacher educators. Changes in the school curricula would be faster in the near future. Corresponding changes in training programmes and strategies shall have to be perceived and given a shape by the teacher educators.

In the context of universalisation of elementary education, teacher educators will be expected to display a deeper understanding of the issues pertaining to access, participation and attainment in their specific regions or areas. They need adequate professional competence to conduct such surveys and studies would reveal the region specific and area specific issues and problems which would help the functionaries of the education department and the community. They will prepare the trainees in responding to these issues during the training period and also in schools subsequently.

The professional quality of teacher educator will determine the quality of the training of teachers, both pre-service as well as in-service. The professional level at which teachers are prepared would, in turn, determine the quality of school education. Again, teacher educators have to be fully familiar with the school realities, social environment and community expectations to realistically perform the challenging tasks before them. On the professional side, teacher educators need to be actively associated with policy formulations, implementation strategies and monitoring of programmes.

In India, the only programme which is often treated as preparing teacher educators is that of M.Ed. Scrutiny of the curriculum of most of the M.Ed. programmes would reveal that these have not been specifically designed to prepare teacher educators. There are some M.Ed. programmes where provisions do not exist for writing a dissertation. The products of these programmes would certainly not be in a position to conduct research, initiate innovation on their own and induct teacher trainees in these areas which are essential functions of teacher educators. Prior to the establishment of the NCTE as a statutory body, NCERT acted as its secretariat and organised several professional development programmes for teacher educators in areas like micro-teaching and simulation, student teaching and evaluation, preparing research proposals, improvement of teacher education curricula and so on.

The University Grants Commission (UGC) has been organising national and regional level workshops for improvement of the teacher education programmes. Through various schemes it offers financial support for seminars, workshops and research projects for teacher educators for such themes as higher education, educational technology, non-formal education, population education, environmental education, research methodology, etc.

The National Institute of Educational Planning and Administration (NIEPA) organises programmes for Principals of Colleges of Education, Heads of University Departments of Education and other administrators concerned with teacher education. The SCERTs and State Boards of Teacher Education organise continuing education programmes for teacher educators on teaching methodologies for new subject areas and on innovations in education.

Some University Departments of Education organise seminars, workshops, and orientation programmes for teacher educators on teaching, development of instructional skills, interaction analysis, teaching behaviour, educational technology, guidance and counselling and research methodology. Certain Colleges of Education and University Departments of Education have been upgraded as Colleges of Teacher Education (CTEs) and Institutions of Advanced Study in Education (IASEs) for taking up innovations in teacher education.

NCTE after its establishment in 1995 as a statutory body, has initiated several programmes aimed at enhancing professional competence of teacher educators. These include seminars and workshops in the area of human rights and national values, indigenous thoughts in education, indigenous approach to teacher preparation, institutional networking and capacity enhancement and production of good quality enrichment materials for teacher educators. These institutions have considerable experiences in organising training and development activities. Based upon the experience gained they will have to evolve programmes of sequential nature with in-built mechanism for assessment and impact evaluation.

In the absence of an appropriate policy of recruitment, specially at the pre-primary, primary and elementary stages of teacher preparation, the manpower in the institutions of teacher education does not necessarily possess the professionally required qualifications for the preliminary stages.

At the pre-primary stage one comes across teacher educators who have passed high school or higher secondary examination and possess a certificate in teacher training, not necessarily meant for the pre-primary stage; graduates or those with higher qualification with absolutely no training background or with the background not appropriate for that stage or level.

As regards the primary and elementary stages, the teacher educators, generally, possess graduate or higher qualification with teacher training mostly at the B.Ed. level. There are serious lacunae in the recruitment policies in as much as the professional qualifications prescribed are not stage-specific and mostly not suited to the education of teachers for the stage or level concerned. This situation calls for fresh thinking regarding recruitment policies for teacher educators and well-planned programmes of education for teacher educators.

Education and training of teacher educators has to focus its attention on the new role of teacher educators on the problems which reflect the emerging global trends in education and the overall needs and aspirations of the people in India. It has also to deal with specific problems confronting teacher education institutions and to make teacher education more responsible and responsive. It also has to encourage teacher educators' continuing professional growth.

In addition, there are certain practical problems as well. For instance , what would be the basic qualifications of teacher educators at various stages of teacher preparation? What would be the requirements in respect of the core education courses and for the organisation of procedures and practices in the institutions. Answers to several of such issues have to be sought in the very rationale of providing professional education.The rationale behind the education and professional training of teacher educators lies in providing qualitative instruction through well-designed programmes of professional education.

The following questions are relevant for designing a programme for education of teacher educators:

— What exactly should the education of teacher educators aim at?

— What are the significant issues and problems concerning the education of teacher educators?

— What are the possible models of both pre-service as well as inservice education of teacher educators?

— What patterns, contents and techniques are envisaged?

— What are the possible agencies and organisations which could be profitably employed in providing continuing abd recurrent inservice education to teacher educators?

The following objectives can be comprehensively identified for the programmes of preparation of teacher educators :

— to develop competencies and skills needed for preparation of teachers and teacher educators

— to enable them to organise competency-based and commitment oriented professional programmes

— to enable them to develop pedagogy relevant to the education of teacher educators

— to acquire an understanding of the needs and problems of teacher educators and teacher education institutions

— to develop skills related to management of teacher education institutions

— to develop competencies of curriculum development and preparation of learning and evaluation materials

— to enable teacher educators to acquire capabilities to organise in-service continuing education programmes

— to enable them to organise need-based and commitment oriented on the job training

— to develop competencies for evaluating educational programmes and teaching learning materials

- — to develop the capacity of examination, analysis, interpretation, elaboration and communication of educational ideas
- — to relate education and the national needs and develop critical awareness about Indian realities
- — to enable them to understand the relationship between Indian ethos, modern technology and education
- — to promote the global perspective of educational development with special reference to the developing countries.
- — to enable them to undertake meaningful educational research.
- — to develop the capacities to reinterpret Indian heritage, culture and values to meet the requirements of the present-day Indian society.
- — to develop the capabilities for self-directed and life-long learning.
- — to enable them to appreciate and adopt emerging communication technology and innovative practices in Indian context.

The present system of pre-service education of teacher educators is characterised by lack of perspective in terms both of contents as well as qualifications. For instance, while it is well accepted that the B.Ed. qualification entitles a person to teach at secondary stage, it is doubtful if the M.Ed. programme adequately prepares a person to become teacher of secondary school teachers. The existing M.Ed. programme has little provision of training in and working out teaching and evaluation strategies suited to the needs of teacher trainees. And yet one finds M.Ed. degree holders entrusted with the responsibility of teacher preparation not only at secondary stage but also at the pre-primary, primary and elementary stages of teacher preparation.

Likewise, while the B.Ed. qualification legitimately entitles a person to teach at the secondary stage, it cannot, at the same time, be accepted as a good enough qualification for being a teacher educator at the primary stage. The existing B.Ed. programme is designed mainly to teach high school students and not for preparing primary school teacher educators. Thus, it is imperative that the professional qualification of teacher educators is made stage-specific suited to the needs of teacher trainees of different categories.

Education of teacher educators has necessarily to correspond to teacher preparation programmes. It is nonetheless necessary to consider alternatives and institute programmes like M.Ed. (Teacher Education) catering to the needs of stage-specific and category-specific preparation of teacher educators alongside general M.Ed. programmes. Existing M.Ed. courses in Indian Universities are by and large academic in nature and not adequately professional in content. In as much as the Master's level courses in Education need to be formulated for making it a professional course, some additional areas of study will have to be introduced with changed orientation.The course structure in respect of the above alternative M.Ed programmes has to correspond to the course structure of teacher education at various stages and categories. For instance, the M.Ed (Elementary) programme may comprise the following courses.

The preparation of teacher educators would concern itself with the relevant theoretical courses as well as the consonant practicum. At the theoretical level, the choice of pedagogical inputs has to be guided by various contexts and their educational and professional concerns. In addition to theory courses, specialisation courses with reference to teacher education have to be included. The theoretical courses will have a bearing on the practice of teacher education. It will be necessary to develop competencies and skills in prospective teacher educators relating to their work situations. What goes on in teacher training institutions by way of educational programmes and activities has to be reflected in the education and training of teacher educators. It essentially implies that the preparation of teacher educators has to be made an integral part of the system of teacher education.

It will be pertinent to evolve a pedagogy relevant to the stage or category specific programmes. It will lay due emphasis on societal goals, values specially those enshrined in the Indian Constitution, higher order learning processes, curriculum development and theory and practice of educational research including action research. Competence to carry out research and innovations needs to be acquired by all. Training in curriculum development and preparation of learning materials is inalienable aspect of entire process of teacher education. Similarly, development of evaluation materials would result into more effective utilisation of evaluation in teacher education institutions.

The practical work has among other things necessarily to include internship programme by way of attachment to the stage-specific and category-specific teacher education institutions. This will give the prospective teacher educators an adequate knowledge of the total functioning of teacher education institution, the improvements needed and also provide insights into the problems and issues concerning maintenance of institutional plant, classroom management, organisational climate of the institution etc.

As for practice teaching, the main thrust has to be on a variety of techniques such as team teaching, micro-teaching, panel discussion, seminar, demonstration, etc. as integral part of classroom-teaching-learning-evaluation procedures. Practical work other than internship and practice teaching has to develop competencies and skills in organising activities concerning work education and working with community as per the practical work requirements in the teacher education institutions.

10

Teacher Evaluation

Teacher evaluation systems are deemed by most school administrators and teachers to be extremely stressful, of little or no value, and a barrier to high staff morale. This report provides a review of the literature with a list of criteria and recommendations for an effective teacher evaluation process. Ineffective teacher evaluation systems are more costly than effective ones. Shoddy teacher evaluation programs, because they neither improve teachers' instructional skills nor permit the dismissal of incompetent teachers, rob children of the achievements,, when well-taught, they have the potential to obtain . Conventional teacher evaluation, warns Barth, often resembles a meaningless ritual.

Teacher evaluation is a complex process. It is a series of activities and actions that are interconnected and relate to a specific purpose. Since teachers deal with complex problems, they should be evaluated as professionals which means that their standards should be developed by their peers and their evaluation should focus on the degree to which they solve professional problems competently. The emphasis of their evaluation should be on their teaching and not on them as individuals and take into consideration the involvement and responsiveness of others involved in the education process.

The evaluation process usually involves preparation, observation, data collection, reporting, and follow-up. Data collection normally entails a formal observation which is preceded by a pre-conference and followed by a post-conference. The utilization of formal observations does not mean informal observations are ignored. Many unannounced visits usually prove to be more effective than a few announced visits. However. there are limitations to classroom observations as an assessment method.

Teacher evaluations should be dialogical rather than hierarchical. The division of labour between those who determine what is to be taught and when and how it is to be taught and those who teach must be addressed, because teacher-proofing curriculum and instructional strategies is in direct opposition to treating teachers as professionals. Evaluators should know the subject matter, pedagogy, and classroom characteristics of the teacher being evaluated, as well as take into consideration the fact that experienced and excellent teachers are capable of pedagogical performances that educational theory and research can neither explain nor predict.

These risk-takers and innovators must be encouraged not stifled. Consequently, any effort to define standards for teaching and to operationalize them in an evaluation must reach beyond the judgment of academic experts. Therefore, we need a form of evaluation that will reflect a more enlightened view of teaching, that will inspire teacher educators to aim higher in creating their curricula and designing their pro grams, and that will, in the very process of being implemented through supervised residencies in the schools, introduce new forms of mentoring, collaboration, and collegiality.

The general purpose of teacher evaluation is to safeguard and improve the quality of instruction received by students so boards must provide a process that allows and encourages supervisors and teachers to work together to improve and enhance classroom instructional practices. According to the literature there are six main purposes of teacher evaluation.

1. It should strive to improve instruction by fostering self-development and peer assistance.
2. Staff development activities can be rated and identified
3. The selection process can be validated.
4. A well-designed, properly functioning teacher evaluation process provides a major communication link between the school system and teachers.
5. Personnel decisions such as retention, transfer, tenure, promotion, demotion, and dismissal can be enhanced through an effective evaluation process.
6. Teacher evaluation is capable of protecting students from incompetent teachers by bringing structured assistance to marginal teachers.

Although incompetent teachers may constitute only 2-3% of the teaching force, they tarnish the reputation of the entire profession, shortchange many students, and engender parental dissatisfaction with the public schools. However, the diKculties which incompetent teachers experience in the classroom often stem from multiple causes:

1. the personal shortcomings of the teacher,
2. non-job related influences, and
3. the limitations or failings of supervisors.

Administrators are obligated to confront poor teacher performance. Poor performance is marked by excess:

1. excessive lack of preparation;
2. excessive deficiencies of teaching skills;
3. excessive problems of student control;
4. excessive manifestations of poor judgment; and
5. excessive absence from school.

If a teacher does not meet minimal accountability standards, he or she should enter an intensive assistance program. An agreement between the teacher and supervisor, in which the teacher agrees to improve and the supervisor agrees to provide resources to help the teacher improve, should be the first step of the intensive assistance program. Conley states that the dismissal mode is reached only after effort has first been made to remediate the individual's performance because unemployment detrimentally affects the welfare of an employee and his/her dependents.

Teaching malpractice continues to victimize students by wasting their opportunities to learn, society by failing to provide a service for which it paid, teachers by perpetuating their failures, and the teaching profession by diluting quality, contaminating its ranks, and tarnishing its image, thus causing it to lose its political power.

Various models of teacher evaluation have been offered. McGreal categorizes them into four main models: Common Law, Goal Setting, Product, and Artistic or Naturalistic. Gitlin dk Smyth neatly package them into two main categories: educative and dominant, with Walsh calling them participative and controlling. Gitlin and Smyth would classify McGreal's Common Law, Goal Setting, and Product models as dominant and Walsh would classify them as controlling because they are individually focused, judgmental, and hierarchical. Processes of evaluation like those promoted by people like Madeline Hunter, that make lavish claims to being scientific and research-based, are really nothing more than ways of "bolstering corporate, institutional, and bureaucratic interests". "I tried to follow the letter and spirit of 'The Hunter Model' as we trudged through each part of our teacher evaluation system, hut it just wasn't working". By concentrating exclusively on the technical aspects of good teaching, they divert attention away from "an analysis of the economic, social, and political hierarchies that maintain and perpetuate inequality and injustice".

Moving involvement in teacher evaluation beyond individual teachers means that the evaluation of teachers can be shifted from one of blaming the teacher for educational problems to a circumstance in which the wider community begins to accept its legitimate responsibility and role in setting, debating, and monitoring the agenda, norms, and goals of schools. The educative and participative model, if used wisely, could reduce the need for dominant, accountability forms of teacher evaluation.

It is no longer acceptable to judge teaching ability according to a set of pre- determined criteria. Twenty-first century conceptions of school reform and the professionalization of teaching cannot co-exist with early twentieth-century models of evaluation, especially when these afford unacceptably simplistic notions of teaching. The true test of approaches to evaluation will be whether or not they contribute to the needed reforms of teaching and teacher education. If evaluation does not become part of the solution, then it surely will become part of the problem.

Types of Evaluation

There are mainly five main types of evaluation: formative, summative, diagnostic, criterion and normative.

— *Formative evaluation*: It is an ongoing classroom process that keeps the students and educators informed of students' progress. The main purpose of formative evaluation is to improve instruction. This type of evaluation helps the teachers understand the degree to which students are learning the course material and the extent to which their knowledge, understanding, skills, and attitudes are developing. Students are provided direction for future learning and are encouraged to take responsibility for their own progress.

— *Summative evaluation*: It is a type of evaluation used at the end of a term, course, or program for purposes of grading, certification, evaluation of progress, or research on the effectiveness of a curriculum, course of study, or educational plan. The essential characteristic of summative evaluation is that a judgment is made about the student, teacher, or curriculum with regard to the effectiveness of learning or instruction, after the learning or instruction has taken place. In fifth-grade arithmetic, for example, summative evaluation would have as its major purpose to determine the degree to which a student can translate word problems into quantitative solutions or his accuracy and rapidity in handling division. Further purposes would be to grade pupils and the report to parents or administrators.

— *Criterion-based evaluation*: Evaluation is criterion-based when it seeks to assess a learner's performance level based on success criteria implicitly or explicitly defined according to the objectives. It does not involve comparing a learner's performance level with other learners' performance levels. It seeks to determine the extent to which goals and objectives targeted by a particular course have been reached.

— *Diagnostic-based evaluation*: Evaluation is diagnostic when it aims at assessing the individual features of learners in relation to the requirements of courses or curricula. Therefore, the goal of diagnostic evaluation is to identify the distinguishing features of the subject targeted by the evaluation as such features may determine the expected results. Diagnostic evaluation may be conducted at the beginning of any new course or curriculum. In such cases, its aim is to ascertain whether the learner has the skills required to enrol for the course. Diagnostic evaluation may also be implemented during or at the end of a particular course.

— *Normative evaluation*: An evaluation is normative when it compares the performances of a particular learner to the performances of the other learners of the same level or class taken as the reference group. The merit-based listing of learners relates to such a normative evaluation. It is important to remember that different assessment techniques are selected or devised to gather information related to how well students are achieving the learning objectives or the curriculum and to the type of learning outcome (knowledge, understanding, skill, attitude, value, or process), the subject area content, the instructional strategies used, the students' levels of development, and the specific purpose of evaluation. It is also important when evaluating student progress to relate it to the Common Essential Learning's, Gender Equity, Resource Based Learning and Aboriginal Perspectives. These program considerations aid in a full understanding of the course presented to them. They should be able to differentiate between bias and non-bias information or information that is leading or not equitable in gender or race. These are important qualities they can be further assessed on.

THE PROCESS OF EVALUATION

Evaluation can be viewed as cyclical process: preparation, assessment, evaluation, and reflection. The evaluation process involves the teacher as a decision maker throughout the four phases.

— *Preparation Phase*. Decisions are made which identify what is to be evaluated, the type of evaluation (formative, summative, or diagnostic) to be used, the criteria against which student learning outcomes will be judged, and the most appropriate assessment techniques with which to gather information on student progress. The teacher's and student's decisions in this phase form the basis for the remaining phases.

— *Assessment Phase*. The teacher identifies information-gathering techniques, constructs or selects instruments, administers them to the student, and collects the information on student learning progress. The teacher continues to make decisions in this phase. The identification and elimination of bias from the assessment techniques and instruments, and the determination of where, when, and how assessments will be conducted are examples of important considerations for the teacher.

— *Evaluation Phase*. The teacher interprets the assessment information and makes judgements about student progress. Based on the judgements or evaluations, teachers make decisions about student learning programs and report on progress to students, parents, and appropriate school personnel.

— *Reflection Phase*. This phase allows the teacher to consider the extent to which the previous phases in the evaluation process have been successful. Specifically, the teacher evaluates the utility and appropriateness of the assessment techniques used. Such reflection assists the teacher in making decisions concerning improvements or modifications to subsequent teaching and evaluation.

All four phases of the evaluation process are included in formative, diagnostic, and summative evaluation.

Formative Evaluation

Formative evaluation is particularly useful for evaluating long-term conflict resolution work in intractable conflicts. In these conflicts, interconnected disputes, with multiple causes and systemic impact, the dynamics, participants, and even issues may change over time, and thus conflict resolution activities need to refocus on the new realities as they emerge. In fact, it may be useful to conduct repeated formative evaluations periodically throughout the life-cycle of a long-term conflict resolution process. At its most basic, f*ormative evaluation* is an assessment of efforts prior to their completion for the purpose of improving the efforts. It is a technique that has become well developed in the education and training evaluation literature.

For conflict resolution efforts addressing intractable conflicts, appropriate formative evaluation can be a powerful part of an intervention strategy. By assessing efforts, and adjusting strategies in response to the assessment, conflict resolution practitioners can better respond to the changes in conflict dynamics that occur in intractable conflicts. Conflict resolution practitioners can thus recalibrate their efforts to better respond to current conflict dynamics, and make other mid-course corrections as necessary. In addition, by monitoring implementation through a formative evaluation, conflict resolution practitioners can also recognize opportunities to fine tune or even redefine their strategies. Finally, by involving the parties in the formative evaluation effort, conflict resolution practitioners can develop additional commitment on the part of participants and funders to conflict resolution.

For conflict resolution work, formative evaluation offers an opportunity to keep everyone on board, and either keep on track or determine when it is necessary to switch tracks. Robert Stakes is quoted as saying, "When the cook tastes the soup, that's formative. When the guests taste the soup, that's summative." Formative evaluation can take many forms. It is most often conducted by the conflict resolution practitioner, but many involve all the stakeholders.

Formative evaluation encourages a process of reflective practice. More specifically, formative evaluation can strengthen conflict management systems in many ways. These include:

— *Rapid feedback*: Primarily, formative evaluation provides *rapid feedback* on the efficacy of conflict management and resolution work. While a project in is progress, a formative evaluation process provides feedback on how the work is going.

— *Documentation*: A formative evaluation process can *document* how conflict management and resolution work is proceeding, what techniques are used, what problems encountered, and what impacts are made in early and middle stages of work.

— *Planning*: Formative evaluations assist with *planning* and allows for revision of or recommitment to plans. Formative evaluation involves a comparison of program implementation with program plans. It also allows for a reconsideration of program goals and plans. When a formative evaluation reveals that a program has diverged from previous plans, those involved in the work can choose to revise plans to take advantage of new opportunities or return to previous plans in order to respond to current realities. Information from formative evaluation can provide input to future planning and implementation, thus forming the project's future.

The rapid feedback, documentation, and planning roles of formative evaluation make formative evaluation a useful component of reflective conflict resolution practice.

There are many evaluation tools — observation, in-depth interviews, surveys, focus groups, analysis, reports, and dialogue with participants, each of which can be part of formative evaluation. Depending on the goals of the formative evaluation, it may emphasize one or more of these tools. Within the range of formative evaluation approaches, there are four main goals for formative evaluation, each of which may be more or less emphasized depending on the program needs. Each of these approaches to formative evaluation are briefly summarized below, with a focus on their applicability to formative evaluation of conflict resolution work in intractable conflicts.

— *Planning evaluation*: Planning evaluation clarifies and assesses a project's plans. Are the goals and timelines appropriate? Are the methods utilized to reach the goals appropriate? In addition, a planning evaluation can lay the groundwork for future formative and summative evaluations by developing indicators and benchmarks. In conflict resolution work, it is often useful to include a planning evaluation component in order to ensure that all stakeholders share common enough visions of the project plans. A planning evaluation can be a form of consensus building amongst those involved in conflict resolution.

— *Implementation evaluation*: An implementation evaluation focuses on the extent to which a program is proceeding according to plan. Information about ways in which a program is not proceeding according to plan can be used to either revise plans or to revise programming. In conflict resolution assessment, implementation evaluation can be a useful component to feed into a planning-focused evaluation. Where work is not proceeding according to plan, participants and facilitators can use an implementation evaluation with a planning focus to ask themselves why things are not going according to plan, and adjust plans or strategies accordingly.

— *Monitoring evaluation*: A monitoring evaluation is usually conducted by an outside evaluator during the course of a program. A funder may choose to monitor implementation of a conflict resolution project by visiting a workshop, checking in with participants, or talking with project personnel. For long-term conflict resolution work, a monitoring evaluation can provide a funder useful reassurance that money is being well spent.

— *Progress evaluation*: A progress evaluation assesses a program's progress. The project's unique goals should serve as a benchmark for measuring progress. Information from a progress evaluation can later be used in a summative evaluation. In conflict resolution work, a progress evaluation might assess attitude change part-way through a multi-year program, providing both feedback on what's working, and evidence of impact early on in a program.

Formative evaluation by itself does not meet the needs of most conflict resolution initiatives. Formative evaluation's focus is on improving work in progress. It should be employed to the extent that it improves work. Formative evaluation is not an end in itself. Funding limitations often limit the intensity of formative evaluations. Where possible, formative evaluations should form part of funding proposals so that appropriate attention can be given to mid-course assessment and mid-course corrections in long-term conflict resolution work.

Finally, it should be acknowledged that, like all evaluations, formative evaluations may yield results that identify fundamental problems with a conflict management or resolution process. For example, when conflict management techniques are used to address a seemingly tractable dispute that is inherently part of an intractable conflict, a formative evaluation of the conflict management initiative might uncover the potential negative impacts of "successful" dispute management. In other words, where one initiative seems successful based on its own goals, formative evaluation could consider even the relevance of the goals themselves, and raise the long-term questions about dynamics which are perpetuating intractability by addressing some issues part-term.

Formative evaluations can be conducted according to varied evaluation methodologies, but should usually incorporate the following considerations:

— Involve multiple stakeholders

— Involve multiple evaluation tools

— Consider plans, implementation, monitoring, and progress.

The particular shape of a formative evaluation will depend on the context, including the program being evaluated and the resources available. A well-developed form of formative evaluation is described in the Action-Evaluation essay. Other forms of formative evaluation may be more appropriate where it is not possible to involve all stakeholders as consistently as is preferable in a full action-evaluation approach. For example, a training team might discuss amongst themselves the progress in their week-long training every evening, but involve the participants in an explicit formative evaluation for a short session in the middle of the training.

Formative evaluation does not need to take over a project and infuse itself into every aspect of the work, but should be incorporated to the extent that it can improve work. Like all types of evaluation, implementing a formative evaluation in a conflict resolution program requires resources. However, these resources can be well-spent when a formative evaluation supports the reflective practice of conflict resolution, particularly in the long-term efforts that so often focus on seemingly intractable conflicts.

Summative Evaluation

Summative Evaluation typically involves the preparation of a formal report outlining the impact of a program. For instance, an evaluation report will typically detail who participated in a program, what activities affected them, and what gains or improvements resulted from their participation. Often this report will include details regarding what prerequisites or conditions are essential or helpful to the replication of the program, program costs and benefits, and disaggregated results showing findings for specific subgroups of participants.

There is no crisp dividing line between formative evaluation and summative evaluation. Much of the information gathered during formative evaluation activities may be reported in formal summative reports, particularly during the early development of new programs, in order to show how the program is responding to challenges and reaching benchmarks and milestones along the way toward intended outcomes. Usually, a compelling case that your program has had a positive impact requires measurement of program targets before, during, and after implementation of the program. This requires careful program planning and early adoption of appropriate data collection methods and a management information database.

Your summative evaluation report is a showcase for outcomes associated with your program, produced independently by a respected research and development institution. NWREL's Evaluation Program maintains a large, expert staff and state of the art facilities for statistical and qualitative analysis, technical writing, and graphic display of findings. In addition to written reports, we can produce a variety of multimedia presentations of your data, suitable for use in slide shows, publication on the world wide web, etc.

Summative evaluation is a judgment about teaching that is used to make a decision a decision about promotion, tenure, or, even, teaching awards. A summative evaluation of teaching attempts to summarize the complex phenomena of teaching. It typically consists of global ratings of teaching, thus, reducing teaching to generalities.An example of summative evaluation is end-of-course student ratings. Student ratings instruments prompt students to rate six to ten aspects of teaching, and they ask students to make an over-all, summarizing judgment of the instruction. Students' ratings are then averaged and given to faculty as summaries of their teaching. The overall summary rating of instruction may even be shared with students and other faculty members. Such ratings are easily compared and then used for making decisions and answering questions of accountability.

Individual faculty members have little control in the traditional summative evaluation process. They usually do not choose the instrument by which they are evaluated; they do not choose the time of the semester at which they are evaluated; nor do they choose the groups of people to whom the results are distributed.

Formative feedback differs from summative evaluation in several ways. In their sourcebook on formative assessment of teaching, Rando and Lenze describe formative feedback as information gathered for the purpose of improving and developing teaching. This information is meant to inform change. The feedback itself must be specific and concrete enough to suggest actions for improvement. It is typically requested well before the end of a semester of teaching, so that the faculty member may use the information to improve teaching in the current course.For example, consider the professor who asks her students, halfway through the semester, to write a few sentences about how the current instruction has promoted or hindered learning. This faculty member has gathered information that she may now use to make teaching and learning more effective. The formative feedback process entails requesting information, making sense of the information, and implementing changes based on the information collected. This process belongs to faculty members.

They are responsible for making all decisions along the way. They may gather, analyze, and react to the information on their own; or they may decide to invite an instructional consultant to assist in this process. In the case of the professor whose students responded in writing to the current instruction, the faculty member chose the method of collecting data and, after reading students' responses, determined which of the issues would be addressed.Several other examples of formative feedback exist. Faculty may opt to conduct classroom assessment for the purpose of improving teaching. They may ask an instructional consultant to videotape their teaching in order to reflect on teaching development. They may even invite trained facilitators to conduct small group "quality control" interviews with students. In all of these examples, only the faculty member who has initiated the formative feedback process need see the results.

The distinctions just drawn between these two concepts exist at the definitional level; but in practice, the two are intertwined. For example, how can faculty's teaching be judged fairly unless they are provided opportunities to improve and develop their teaching? A system that judges teaching without any effort to support the development of good teaching ultimately fails. Before successfully negotiating the co-existence of summative evaluation and formative feedback, at least two issues must be considered.

First, the two must reside in separate offices. If faculty are to trust formative feedback, formative feedback activities must be separated from summative evaluation activities. Consider the junior faculty member who is contemplating a midsemester review of his teaching. Not sure of the value he places on students' feedback, he wants to request that a peer visit his classroom. In order to be trusted, formative feedback must be provided by someone other than his department chair or faculty members who are responsible for his tenure review. Feedback provided by these folks, no matter how helpful and well-intended at the time, could be subconsciously held against the faculty member as examples of "inadequacies" when making summative decisions. Thus, administrators must see to it that the formative activities are in some way shielded from summative evaluation.

Second, summative evaluation must evolve. If a college truly advocates formative feedback, its summative evaluation procedures must not hamper formative efforts. That is, universities cannot uphold two climates at the same time: the punitive climate often associated with summative evaluation precludes the supportive climate necessary for formative feedback. Thus, summative evaluation systems must become more humane.

Two universities have navigated the waters between formative feedback and summative evaluation. Duquesne University added a formative feedback program to an already existing summative evaluation process. The University of Massachusetts added a new summative evaluation system to an already existing formative feedback program. These two cases offer powerful insights about the co-existence of formative feedback and summative evaluation.

Norm-referenced Evaluation

Norm-referenced evaluation is used for large-scale system evaluation, provincial rankings for scholarship and psycho-educational testing for special needs. Norm-referenced evaluation:

— compares one student's achievement to that of other students;

— requires a large reference group for comparison; and

— is based on a normal distribution, which shows how achievement in a particular area is distributed over an entire population.

Norm-referenced evaluation is not meant for classroom evaluation because a classroom does not provide a large enough reference group. Practices that are congruent with a norm-referenced evaluation system such as using a bell curve, natural breaks, or computer programs that rank students, provide percentages, stanines and corresponding letter grades are not compatible with a criterion-referenced evaluation system.

Criterion-referenced Evaluation

Criterion-referenced evaluation is expected for classroom evaluation. From the information collected through assessment activities, teachers evaluate student performance. They use their insight, knowledge about learning and experience with students, along with the specific criteria, to make judgments about student performance in relation to specific learning outcomes. Criterion-referenced letter grades in Grades 4 to 12 indicate students' levels of performance as they relate to the learning outcomes set out in Integrated Resource Packages for each subject, course or grade. Criterion-referenced evaluation:

— compares student achievement and performance to established criteria; and

— provides information that helps students and teachers redirect efforts, practice learning and establish future learning goals.

Planning

— Identify the learning outcomes from the IRPs, IEPs and other specific goals, objectives or purpose for the learning that will be reflected in the unit or lessons.

— Consider what it might look like when the student has met the learning outcomes.

— Identify and analyze the key features, understandings, attributes or qualities that will be demonstrated.

— Establish a preliminary set of criteria and consider ways the students might demonstrate their learning.

Instruction

— Involve the students in the process of refining the criteria. Provide models or examples in order that the students have a clear picture and understanding of the expectations.

— Provide learning opportunities that allow the students to practice and refine their knowledge.

Assessment

— Build a performance scale from the criteria to assist in the collection of assessment information.

— Use the criteria and performance scale to monitor learning and make necessary adjustments to instruction.

— Provide formative feedback to the students.

Evaluation

— Use the criteria for evaluation of the students' performance by comparing the students' performance or demonstration to the criteria and the performance scale.

— Involve the students in self-evaluation and, when appropriate, peer evaluation.

Reporting

— Conference with the students and provide meaningful feedback to support the students' learning.

— Communicate the students' progress to parents.

Criterion-versus Norm-referenced Testing

Many educators and members of the public fail to grasp the distinctions between criterion-referenced and norm-referenced testing. It is common to hear the two types of testing referred to as if they serve the same purposes, or shared the same characteristics. Much confusion can be eliminated if the basic differences are understood. A student's score is usually expressed as a percentage. Student achievement is reported for individual skills. Each individual is compared with other examinees and assigned a score—usually expressed as a percentile, a grade equivalent score, or a stanine. Student achievement is reported for broad skill areas, although some norm-referenced tests do report student achievement for individual skills. The differences outlined are discussed in many texts on testing. The teacher or administrator who wishes to acquire a more technical knowledge of criterion-referenced test or its norm-referenced counterpart, may find the text from which this material was adapted particularly helpful.

Diagnostic Evaluation

The first step to getting appropriate treatment for depression is a physical examination by a physician. Certain medications as well as some medical conditions such as a viral infection can cause the same symptoms as depression, and the physician should rule out these possibilities through examination, interview, and lab tests. If a physical cause for the depression is ruled out, a psychological evaluation should be done, by the physician or by referral to a psychiatrist or psychologist.

A good diagnostic evaluation will include a complete history of symptoms, i.e., when they started, how long they have lasted, how severe they are, whether the patient had them before and, if so, whether the symptoms were treated and what treatment was given. The doctor should ask about alcohol and drug use, and if the patient has thoughts about death or suicide. Further, a history should include questions about whether other family members have had a depressive illness and, if treated, what treatments they may have received and which were effective.

Last, a diagnostic evaluation should include a mental status examination to determine if speech or thought patterns or memory have been affected, as sometimes happens in the case of a depressive or manic-depressive illness. Treatment choice will depend on the outcome of the evaluation. There are a variety of antidepressant medications and psychotherapies that can be used to treat depressive disorders. Some people with milder forms may do well with psychotherapy alone. People with moderate to severe depression most often benefit from antidepressants. Most do best with combined treatment: medication to gain relatively quick symptom relief and psychotherapy to learn more effective ways to deal with life's problems, including depression.

Depending on the patient's diagnosis and severity of symptoms, the therapist may prescribe medication and/or one of the several forms of psychotherapy that have proven effective for depression. Electroconvulsive therapy (ECT) is useful, particularly for individuals whose depression is severe or life threatening or who cannot take antidepressant medication. ECT often is effective in cases where antidepressant medications do not provide sufficient relief of symptoms. In recent years, ECT has been much improved. A muscle relaxant is given before treatment, which is done under brief anesthesia. Electrodes are placed at precise locations on the head to deliver electrical impulses. The stimulation causes a brief (about 30 seconds) seizure within the brain. The person receiving ECT does not consciously experience the electrical stimulus. For full therapeutic benefit, at least several sessions of ECT, typically given at the rate of three per week, are required.

Evaluation Design

To answer any question, you need to carefully plan and execute each step of the process in order to get good answers. All evaluations pose their own special challenges in terms of gathering and analyzing data. When answering descriptive questions, we need to figure out whether the information we need is best gathered through the use of structured or unstructured interviews, focus groups, document analysis, observation, surveys, the use of existing data, or some combination of these and other strategies. Then we need to specify a plan for the data collection and analysis, reporting, and getting the results used. In total, this is the evaluation design. In general, open-ended evaluation approaches work best when we are evaluating a relatively untried intervention, or when the context is very different from other places it has been implemented. An open-ended evaluation design allows for the possibility of gathering information we hadn't anticipated.

When the intervention is something we understand fairly well and have seen implemented in a similar context, we are more likely to have a clear idea of what descriptive data we need. In this case, it makes sense to devise a more structured evaluation approach (e.g., using structured interviews or surveys) that is focused on obtaining very specific information. The reality is that most descriptive evaluation questions fall somewhere between these two extremes - we may have a fairly good idea of what we need to know, but we have learned to expect the unexpected. In such cases, a mix of evaluation approaches (some focused, some open-ended) is best.

Choices about evaluation approaches for normative questions, which compare "what is" with "what should be," follow a similar logic to those for descriptive questions. The added layer of complexity is determining the "what should be" part of the equation. In the simplest cases, there may be a clearly specified goal or target, or some appropriate standards for implementation. In other cases, a needs assessment may be required to identify "what should be." A needs assessment looks at where "dysfunction" (or unsatisfactory functioning) is occurring in the target population or area, as it relates to the intervention. For a farming advisory intervention, you might investigate in what areas and why certain farmers are getting less-than-optimal yields or market prices, and identify the skills, knowledge, and resources that prevent them from achieving better results. In this case, "what should be" might be the level of farming yield and income that could reasonably be achieved, given the right advice and know-how about how to access needed resources.

Impact questions pose the greatest challenge; this is where we need a well thought out design (as opposed to a particular approach to answering a relatively straightforward descriptive question). In any evaluation with questions involving impact, the evaluation design must be able to rule out other feasible explanations for the observed results in order to conclude that the invention had an impact. In other words, we need to be sure that any observed changes were due to the intervention, rather than to something else.

To reduce the possibility of being fooled into thinking we know something as true which really is not, there is much that we can borrow from social science methods. Using experimentation, it is possible to control the implementation of a program, policy, or project, who receives it, and the environment in which it is delivered. When you can control everything but the intervention, you can then be fairly certain that any differences you observe are the result of that intervention.

Supposing you have a fertilizer that is intended to increase the crop yield of corn. Let's say you have a greenhouse where you control the temperature, water, and soil conditions. You create two separate growing areas within the greenhouse and randomly plant the seeds in the testing area and the control area. Both areas receive the same temperature, sunlight, and water and are planted in the exact same soil mixture. The test area receives the fertilizer and the control area does not. At harvest, the yields are measured. If the test area has a higher yield than the control area, you will conclude the fertilizer made a difference.

Now let's think about what happens when you're working in the field instead of the controllable environment of the greenhouse. It is possible that your two areas are close together and the fertilizer can run off into the non-test area, thus giving you an imperfect measure of the impact of the fertilizer. You might move the non-test area to a different part of your field but the soil, light, temperature or rain may be slightly different. The two fields may also receive different amounts of attention. While you can still measure impact, you may be less certain about concluding that the fertilizer alone caused those results.

In the complex world in which development interventions take place, it becomes difficult to identify impact in the midst of other factors. In the agricultural case, let's suppose an irrigation intervention was implemented during a time of ideal weather and strong demand for the crops. The income in the area where the irrigation intervention was implemented increased over prior years. But is the higher income a result of the intervention? Or is it caused by other factors, such as general economic good times or an unusual period of political stability.

Multi-site and cluster evaluations present special challenges as well as unique opportunities for looking at impact questions. The context at each site and the nature of the intervention often vary considerably across different locations.

This can help identify some of the situational and implementation factors that enhance or hinder impact - but the analysis can be considerably more complex. This complexity may limit the extent to which the data collection and analysis phases can be conducted in a highly participatory mode, and it may also limit the viability of rapid assessments as an option. Evaluation designs can help us determine the impact of a program to the extent that they give us control over the implementation and measurement of the program. The intent is to eliminate other possible explanations for what we observe.

Elements of Impact Evaluation Design

To answer whether an intervention made a difference, the evaluation has to show that the key measures changed as a result of the intervention. Before and after measurement is one way to measure change. Change is measured by comparing key measures after the intervention began against the measures taken before the intervention began. The "before" measure might be called a baseline. However, a design with just before and after measures is insufficient to demonstrate that the intervention alone caused the change. Maybe the people changed their behavior because they were being observed or maybe something else occurred at the same time as the intervention that really caused the changes we observed.

It is also important to remember that in a situation where there is little change in the measures, you should be hesitant to conclude that the intervention did not work. An intervention to reduce poverty was implemented in a country. Everyone was eligible to receive the intervention so there was no comparison group. At the end of ten years, the proportion of people in poverty did not change. Can you conclude that the poverty reduction intervention did not work? Without a comparison group, you cannot tell if poverty would have been worse if the poverty reduction intervention was not in place. The intervention may have been effective in holding the line on poverty in spite of declining economic conditions. To strengthen this design, you would want to compare your intervention group to a group who did not receive the intervention.

If an intervention causes change, then those who participate in the intervention will show more change than those who did not. Returning to the irrigation intervention, we would need to compare a similar agricultural area that did not receive the irrigation program with the one that did. If the income in the area that received the irrigation program increased while the income of the comparison group did not, then we would have stronger evidence that the irrigation program caused a positive outcome.

However, not all the other factors have been ruled out. What if the community that receives the irrigation intervention is different in some important ways from the comparison community that did not? Maybe other industries moved into the intervention area, thus increasing income. Or maybe the comparison community grew different crops and their crops did not command as high a price as the crops grown in the irrigation community. In some interventions, there will be those who receive it and those who don't.

This design can be used in evaluation, as might be done in the evaluation of a job training program for laid off workers were more motivated or had more job experience, so it was easier for them to find new employment. To strengthen this design, it is necessary to randomly assign people to participate or not to participate in the program.

In the ideal world of science, we would be able to randomly assign people (or things, farms, roads, cases, whatever) to receive the intervention or not. Random assignment makes the groups comparable. For example, if we randomly assign communities to receive the irrigation intervention or not, we make the groups relatively equal in terms of a variety of factors we cannot control. Given the equality of the groups in terms of a host of factors, we would feel more confident in concluding the intervention had an impact if the intervention group had higher income than the control groups.

However, random assignment is not always an option. Sometimes all eligible people are supposed to receive the intervention, and/or it would be unethical to withhold it from some of them. Sometimes you cannot make people participate in an intervention. In this instance, it may be more practical to provide an intervention in a selection of sites rather than provide interventions in multiple sites and then randomly assign participants.

It is possible, however, to be in a situation where the intervention is not large enough to accommodate all those who apply. A manager might want to assign those with the best chance of benefiting from the intervention to participate. This may be a way to get the most benefit from limited program dollars. For example, the training program is likely to show the best results if it chooses highly motivated people to participate. However, from an evaluation perspective, if the best people are assigned to the program, there is likely to be a bias in the results. Actually, in this type of situation, random assignment may not only enable the use of a strong design to measure impact, it may also be more equitable; no bias and favoritism is in play when assignment is based on chance.

Sometimes it is not possible to randomly assign people to groups for comparison purposes. However, it might be possible to find a group of people who will not be receiving the intervention yet, and who could be used to compare results with. But without random assignment, there is still a good chance that the comparison group differs in important ways from the group receiving the intervention. If that's true, the intervention might look effective simply because of pre-existing differences between recipients and non-recipients. In such cases, one option is to collect data about factors that might be different between the two groups, and that seem likely to impact outcomes. These variables are then built into the data analysis as "control variables." This allows us to rule out some alternative explanations even when random assignment is not possible.

11

PE Teacher Training in India

Physical education is an integral part of Indian education system. It aims at building a sound body, a sharp mind and wholesome personality. It is essential for the cultivation of vitality, courage, self-confidence, coopera-tiveness, leadership, obedience, discipline and positive attitude towards life and the world. The great educational thinkers like Plato, Rousseau, Gandhi, Aurobindo and Russell have laid great emphasis on it. Physical education stresses:

— development of sociability, obedience and discipline, acceptance of authority, positive attitude, equanimity, rapport with others and group consciousness.

— development of emotional stability, control over one's own feelings and temptations.

— development of mental health, ability to take immediate decision and prompt action.

— cultivation of the power of concentration.

— inculcation of democrative values.

— development of neuro-muscular skills

— formation of character and development of willpower.

Development of physical fitness and health of students is not the responsibility of the teachers of physical education alone. In fact, every teacher has a role to play in this direction, especially at the elementary stage and must have substantial exposure to physical education and health education. The teachers other than physical education teachers also need to take interest in games and sports and physical activities.

Every prospective teacher irrespective of the level needs to be made conversant with the basics of physical education. In addition, every trainee is required to participate in at least one major group game and two items of sports. It needs to be provided for in the curriculum with a view to enabling them to generate a climate for promotion of physical activities.

Curriculum for Physical Education should be viewed from the following two angles:

a) Physical education as an integral part of teacher education programmes at all levels.

b) Physical education specifically for preparing teachers of physical education.

OBJECTIVES

The objectives of physical education as an integral part of teacher education may be as follows:

— to enable teachers to be conversant with the basics of physical education

— to enable them to understand the relationship between general education and physical education

— to enable them to organise games and sports and physical activities

The expected outcome of such an approach will lead to universalisation of physical education activities in schools.

STRATEGIES

— Inclusion of physical education component in teacher education at all levels.

— Compulsory participation in at least one major group game and two items of sports.

TEACHERS OF PHYSICAL EDUCATION AT ELEMENTARY STAGE

These courses leading to a certificate or diploma are being suggested for the teachers of physical education at the elementary stage. The programme aims at realising the following objectives:

Objectives

— to enable prospective teachers to understand the nature and purpose of physical education at elementary stage

— to develop among the students awareness of basic principles of health, hygiene and nutrition

— to enable them to develop good health and sound physique of students

— to foster interest in physical exercises, games and sports

— to inculcate the spirit of healthy competition and leadership

— to develop team spirit and fellow feeling

— to promote among them the competencies for organizing different kinds of activities in physical education

— to enable them to develop among students the physical and mental alertness

— to enable them to develop emotional stability and self-control

Curriculum Framework

Theory

— Emerging Indian Society

— Physical Education : principles, purpose, status, problems and issues

— Psychology and Sociology of Physical Education

— Methods and Techniques of Physical Education
— Basics of Anatomy, Physiology and Kinesiology
— Health and Safety Education
— Management and Organization of Physical Education
— Yoga - basics of theory and practices

Practice Teaching and Practicals

— Demonstration
— Coaching
— Organization of games and sports
— Organization of indigenous and local games and sports
— Organization of community games and sports
— Lessons in Yogic exercises
— First aid, care of minor injuries, bandage and massage
— Upkeep and use of materials and equipment
— Marching
— Swimming
— Gymnastics
— Relaxation exercises

TEACHERS OF PHYSICAL EDUCATION AT THE SECONDARY STAGE

B.P.Ed. programme is intended to prepare the teachers of physical education for the secondary schools. The programme aims at realising the following objectives :

— to enable teachers to understand the nature, purpose and philosophy of physical education at the secondary stage
— to prepare teachers of physical education with broader educational perspective
— to develop potentialities for planning and organising physical education programmes and activities

— to develop capacity to organize leisure and recreational activities

— to empower them to inspire their students to actively participate in physical and yogic exercises, games and sports

— to enable teachers to develop personality, character, will-power, democratic values and positive attitude towards life among their students

— to make teachers capable of imparting basic knowledge about health, hygiene and nutrition

— to develop skills and competencies to organise school and community games and sports

— to cultivate the spirit of sportsmanship, mental and physical alertness, scientific temper and optimism

— to promote mental health, power of self-decision and self-control, correct judgement and action, emotional stability and equanimity, respect for others and acceptance of authority and rules

— to promote appreciation and interest for indigenous games, sports and yogic exercises.

— to create awareness about health and hygiene in the community.

Curriculum Framework

Theory

— Emerging Indian Society

— Foundations of Physical Education

— Management of Physical Education, Games and Sports

— Kinesiology and Physiology of Exercises

— Anatomy, Physiology and Health Education

— Psychology and Physical Education

— Guidance and Counselling in Physical Education
— Evaluation in Physical Education
— Adapted Physical Education

Specialization

— Sports Medicine
— Rules of Games and Sports
— Science of Training and Coaching
— Yogic Education and Indigenous Games
— Education of Athletes

Practicals and Practice Teaching

— Demonstration
— Practice of Coaching
— Organization of Games, Sports and Recreational Activities
— Organisation of Meets/Camping
— Participation and Training in major games and sports
— Participation and training in major indigenous games and sports and yogic exercises
— Track and Field Events
— Gymnastics and Tumbling
— Marching and Calisthenics
— Defensive Martial Arts
— Aquatics
— First aid, bandage and massages
— Care and Management of minor injuries
— Conditioning Exercises
— Relaxation Exercises

MASTERS COURSE IN PHYSICAL EDUCATION

The Masters programme is intended to prepare teacher educators for physical education. Its objectives may be the following :

— to enable prospective teacher educators to understand the nature, purpose and philosophy of physical education

— to develop competencies necessary for physical training and coaching

— to develop knowledge, skills and competencies necessary for imparting physical education

— to enrich knowledge of personal and community health

— to promote the capacity to organise games, sports and recreational activities

— to provide knowledge of sports medicine and physiotherapy

— to develop competence to undertake research in physical education, games and sports

— to enable them to prepare good athletes

— to inculcate the spirit of sportsmanship

— to foster interest in physical education and appreciate its role in school and society

— to prepare for evolving stage-specific curriculum, pedagogy and evaluation techniques in physical education

— to develop an understanding and appreciation of indigenous approach to physical education, exercises, games and sports

Curriculum Framework

Theory

— Emerging Indian Society

- Physical Education in Historical, Philosophical and Social Perspectives
- Psychology and Physical Education
- Physiology of Exercises
- Curriculum Development in Physical Education
- Evaluation in Physical Education
- Mechanical and Scientific Principles of Coaching
- Research Methods in Physical Education

Specialization

- Management of Physical Education, Games and Sports
- Sports Medicine
- Physiotherapy
- Principles and Practice of yogic exercises and Indigenous games and sports
- Training Methods : Exercises, Games and Sports
- Rules and regulations of games and sports

Dissertation/project work

Practical Work

- Demonstration
- Advanced Coaching
- Organization of games and sports meets, camps and recreational activities
- Tests - Development, administration and scoring
- Sports Skills tests
- Major Fitness tests
- Strength tests
- General Motor Ability tests

— Psychomotor tests
— Cardiovascular tests
— National Physical Fitness tests
— Physiotherapy
— Dislocation Reduction
— Yogic therapy
— Hydrotherapy
— Electrotherapy
— Relaxation
— Massage
— Bandaging
— First Aid and Care for Minor Injuries
— Reconditioning

Transaction and Evaluation

Detailed curriculum planning will accord due considertion to region or area specific practices and approaches to transactional strategies. Explanation, demonstration, participation, performance and evaluation would be major components of transcational strategies. Corrective measures and remediation inputs would flow from evaluation leading to attainment of levels of performance. Group evaluation and community appreciation would provide much needed motivation to both the teachers and trainees.

Institutions and Programmes

Establishment of National College of Physical Education

The National College of Physical Education which has now been named the Lakshmibai College of Physical Education after the late Rani Lakshmibai of Jhansi started functioning at Gwalior from 17th August, 1957. The College that is situated in a campus of about 150 acres, is the only institution of its kind in the country and will provide training facilities for a three-year degree course in Physical education at the under-graduate level. It will ultimately develop into a national centre for post-graduate studies and research in Physical education. Pending the construction of its own buildings the College has started functioning in the buildings of the former Race Course at Gwalior.

Initially the College started with 30 admissions that will pro- gressively increase. The ultimate aim is to admit 100 students every year. Although a coeducational institution only men students have been admitted this year. A Syllabus for a three-year degree course has also since been finalised.

The Government of India have earmarked a total provision of Rs. 70 lakhs to meet non-recurring as well as recurring expenditure on the college during the Second Five-Year Plan period. Grants amounting to Rs. 1,69,126 have been paid so far to the Board of Governors of the College during 1957-58 to meet the expenditure on the College during the year.

For 1958-59 a budget provision of Rs. 17.64 lakhs has been made for the College, out of which Rs. 12 lakhs are earmarked for the construction of the College buildings. The construction work of the College buildings has been entrusted to the Central Public Works Department.

For purposes of administration and control, the college has been placed under an autonomous Board of Governors with a Chairman nominated by the Government of India.

Scheme for the Promotion of Physical Education under Second Five- Year Plan

On the basis of the recommendations of the Central Advisory Board, of Physical Education and Recreation, the Government of India have included the following schemes in their educational development programme under the Second Five-Year Plan with a total provision of Rs. 40 lakhs over the Plan period for these Schemes:

(i) Strengthening of Institutions and Colleges of Physical Education.

(ii) Implementation of the Syllabuses of Physical Education for Boys and Girls (from Primary to Higher Secondary stage) prepared by the Central Advisory Board of Physical Education and Recreation.

(iii) Promotion of Research in Physical Education.

(iv) Popularisation of Norms of Physical Efficiency Tests.

(v) Conducting Seminars on Physical Education for Physical Educationists,

(vi) Award of Visiting Fellowships.

(vii) Award of Scholarships for Higher Studies in Physical Education.

(viii) Financial Assistance to Vyayamshalas and Akadas.

(ix) Miscellaneous measures e.g., Publication of literature, Celebration of National Physical Efficiency Weeks and Days, National Festival of Physical and Recreational Activities, Production of Documentary and Feature Films on Physical Education etc.

All these schemes have been forwarded to all State Governments/ Union Territories and the Physical Education Training Institutions with the request that proposals for financial assistance under the schemes may be forwarded to this Ministry. There has been quite a good response from the State Governments and the Universities for proposals for financial assistance.

Reconstitution of Central Advisory Board of Physical Education and Recreation

The Central Advisory Board of Physical Education and Recreation has been reconstituted. The first meeting of the reconstituted Board was held on 31-1-58. The Board, it may be added, had been set up by the Government of India in 1950 to advise on the coordination of all programmes and activities in the field of Physical Education and Recreation, but, had been held in abeyance on account of financial stringencies and was revived in 1953. The Board functioned till December, 1956 when the Government decided to reconstitute it so as to make it more broadbased.

In pursuance of one of the recommendations of the Central Advisory Board of Physical Education and Recreation as contained in the National Plan of Physical Education and Recreation, the State Governments and the Universities have been requested in a circular letter to set up State and University Boards of Physical Education and Recreation with powers and functions similar to the Central. Advisory Board of Physical Education and Recreation.

Recognition of Diplomas and Certificates of Physical Education Training Institutions

The Central Advisory Board of Physical Education and Recreation had prepared Rules for the Recognition of Diplomas and Certificates of Physical Education Training Institutions in the country. The Board had; also set up a Committee of its own to scrutinize the diplomas and certificates of Physical Education Training Institutions in this connection.

The Committee in its report has recommended that for a proper assessment of the Diploma and Certificate courses offered by the various institutions for purposes of their recognition by the Government of India, an 'on-the-spot' study of the various institutions by an Inspecting Team would be necessary. This recommendation of the Committee has been accepted by the Government and an Inspecting Team of the Government is proposed to be sent out for an 'on-the-spot" study of the various institutions.

An exhaustive questionnaire has been sent out by the Government to the institutions in this connection. The information collected through the questionnaire will be utilised by the Inspecting Team during their 'on-the-spot' study of the institutions concerned.

Sports: The programme of holding Coaching Camps which was initiated in October, 1955 was continued during the period under report and Coaching Camps in Basketball, Volleyball, Badminton and Wrestling have been conducted in which nearly 80 teachers/ physical instructors drawn from educational institutions in the country received training in the method and technique of the game. Before the close of the year coaching camps in Table Tennis, Hockey, Cricket, Football, Athletics, Kabaddi and Swimming are, proposed to be held.

A new experiment, namely, coaching camps on regional basis, is proposed to be initiated during this winter. On an experiment basis, it has been decided to hold Regional Coaching Camps in Cricket, Athletics and Football at Madras, Bombay and Delhi respectively during the months of February and March, 1958 and if the experiment proves successful more such camps will be held.

For the promotion of Sports and Games in the country, grants have been paid to the National Sports Federation amounting to Rs. 58,538/9/-. A sum of Rs. 2,58,380 has been paid to the U.P. Council of Sports for the construction of a Sports Stadium at Lucknow and another sum of Rs. 45,000 has been paid to Mysore Government for the construction of a Guest House.

For the better coordination and organization of Sports activities paid Secretaries have been appointed to the following National Sports Organizations/State Councils of Sports:

(a) Indian Hockey Federation;

(b) Badminton Association of India;

(c) Basketball Federation of India;

(d) National Rifle Association;

(e) U.P. Council of Sports; and

(f) Kerala Sports Council.

On the lines of the All-India Council of Sports, State Councils of Sports have been set up in the States of Assam, Bombay, Kerala, Madras, Rajasthan, Uttar Pradesh, Andhra, Bihar, West Bengal and in the Centrally administered areas of Delhi and the Andaman and Nicobar Islands.

Rajkumari Sports Coaching Scheme

The Rajkumari Sports Coaching Scheme was inaugurated in September, 1953. The Scheme during the five years of its operation has made the country coaching conscious, established permanent coaching centres, offered coaching assistance to various State centres in almost all sports-outdoor and indoor—and organised coaching of coaches with the help of foreign coaching personnel. During this year it has concentrated mostly on the Youth of India by organising Coaching Camps at University and School Centres. A grant of Rupees three lakhs was made up to December 1957 and a grant of Rupees two lakhs is expected to be released by the end of the financial year 1957-58. It is proposed to organise coaching in Athletics, Tennis, Circket, Hockey, Football, Badminton, Table Tennis, Basketball, Volleyball, Swimming and Gymnastics at a total cost of Rupees five lakhs during 1958-59.

Bharat Scouts and Guides

In order to help the expansion of the movement in the country, the Government of India have sanctioned grants to the tune of Rs. 1,58,561 during 1957-58. This figure includes a grant-in-aid of Rs. 74,448 given to the National Head- quarters of Bharat Scouts and Guides for meeting 50% of the cost on return airfare of 47 Scouts and guides, who participated in the Jubilee Scouts Jamboree and World Camp of Girl Guides held at London in July-August) 1957. A grant-in-aid of Rs. 9,113 was also sanctioned for sending a contingent of Girl Guides to participate in the Philippines Jamboree.

With a view to establishing a permanent all-India Training Centre at Pachmarhi for training of Scout-Masters and others, the National Headquarters of Bharat Scouts and Guides have submitted a proposal requesting the Government of India for financial assistance. The request is under consideration.

Health Education

With a view to implementing the suggestion of Indian Delegation that attended the Joint Seminar organised by W.H.O./F.A.O., in Baguio (Philippine Islands) in October, 1955, the Government of India have set up a Committee on Health Education and Nutrition Education with effect from 16th December, 1957.

National Discipline Scheme

The National Discipline Scheme that has the object of imparting physical and moral discipline to children has been taken over from the Ministry of Rehabilitation by this Ministry in December, 1957. As implemented by the Ministry of Rehabilitation the Scheme is in force only in schools for displaced children in certain parts of Northern India. It is now proposed to extend the scope of the scheme to schools other than those for displaced children in three regions of the country corresponding to Bombay, Bengal and the Punjab. Shri J. K. Bhonsle has been appointed Adviser for the implementation of the National Discipline Scheme. The scheme will be implemented in 195 schools during 1957-58 and 1958-59. This figures is expected to rise to 300 during 1960-61.

Youth Welfare

After the recent cut imposed on the entire Plan provision, a sum of Rs. 70 lakhs was provided for Youth Welfare Schemes for the Second Plan period. A sum of Rs. 6.66 lakhs was earmarked for this programme for the year 1957-58. A brief account of the progress on these schemes is as follows:

Student's Tours

Under this programme the Government of India render financial assistance to schools and colleges for organising educational tours for small batches of students. The grant is to the extent of 75% of the railway/bus fare at students' concessional rates. Organised tours have become popular with the students. During the current financial year a sum of Rs. 1,49,475 has already been sanctioned for the benefit of about 5,207 students and teachers of 170 institutions. A sum of Rs. 2,00,000 has been provided for the year 1958-59 for this scheme out of the total Plan provision of Rs. 10 lakhs.

Inter-University and Inter-Collegiate Youth Festivals

The Fourth Inter-University Youth Festival was held from 1st to 10th November, 1957 at New Delhi. Sixteen hundred students from 38 universities participated.

The Fourth Festival has been the biggest in the series conducted so far; the number of participants was the largest and arrangements were more elaborate than those made in previous years. The duration of the festival was also increased from seven to 10 days. Several additional features were introduced in the recent festival, by way of an additional theatre, club room facilities and increased facilities for accommodation, sanitary conveniences etc. Another important feature of this year's festival was that the programme included Symposia on subjects of general interest to students in addition to competitions in Drama, Dance, Music and Elocution and an Arts and Crafts Exhibition.

Bibliography

Brewer, Jo. *The Biggest Little Games Book Ever!: For Teachers and Community Leaders Everywhere*. The Creative Network, 1991.

Eichstaedt, Carl B. and Leonard H. Kalakian. *Developmental/Adapted Physical Education: Making Ability Count. 3rd ed.*. Macmillan, 1993. 672 p.

Eshuys, Joe, et al. *Fundamentals of Health and Physical Education*. The Jacaranda Press, 1987.

Franks, B. Don and Edward T. Howley. *Fitness Facts: The Healthy Living Handbook*. Human Kinetics, 1989. 181 p.

Getchell, Bud. *Physical Fitness: A Way of Life. 4th ed.* Macmillan, 1992. 368 p.

Graham, George. *Teaching Children Physical Education: Becoming a Master Teacher*. Human Kinetics, 1992. 179 p.

Greenberg, Jerrold S. and David Pargman. *Physical Fitness: A Wellness Approach. 2nd ed.*. Prentice-Hall, 1989. 350 p.

Kamiya, Art. Parker, *Elementary Teacher's Handbook of Indoor & Outdoor Games*. 1985. 224 p.

Kotnour, Mary. *Physical Fitness Games and Activities Kit*. Parker Publishing, 1990. 285 p.

Morris, G.S. Don and Jim Stiehl. *Changing Kids' Games*. Human Kinetics, 1989. 144 p.

Mosston, Muska and Sara Ashworth. *Teaching Physical Education. 4th ed.*. Maxwell Macmillan, 1994. 268 p.

Pangrazi, Robert P. and Douglas N. Hastad. *Physical Fitness in the Elementary Schools*. AAHPERD, 1989.

Phillip, Joan A. and Jerry D. Wilkerson. *Teaching Team Sports: A Coeducational Approach*. Human Kinetics, 1990. 303 p.

Province of British Columbi, *Physical Education Active Health: Resource Book Levels I-V*. 1987. 227 p.

R. D. Berry. *Sports Therapy Taping Guide*. Kennedy, Sports-Medics, 1991. 115 p.

Rev. ed.. Stewart, Gordon W. and Robert A. Faulkner. *Bend and Stretch: Suppleness and Strength Exercises.* 3S Fitness Group, 1984. 31 p.

Schurr, Evelyn. *Movement Experiences for Children. 3rd ed.*. Prentice- Hall, 1980. 578 p. I

Seaton, Don, et al. *Physical Education Handbook*. Prentice-Hall, 1992.

Sherrill, Claudine. Wm. C. Brown, *Adapted Physical Education and Recreation: A Multi-Disciplinary Approach. 3rd ed.* 1986. 656 p.

Strand, Bradford N. and Rolayne Wilson. *Assessing Sports Skills*. Human Kinetics, 1993. 165 p.

Thomas, Jerry R., Amelia M. Lee and Katherine T. Thomas.*Physical Education for Children: Concepts Into Practice*. Human Kinetics, 1988. 256 p.

Wetton, Pauline. *Bright Ideas: Games for Physical Education*. Scholastic, 1987. 127 p.

Wheeler, Keg and Otto H. Spiker. *Physical Education Curriculum Activities Kit for Grades K-6*. Parker Publishing, 1991. 272 p.

Index